The New York Times

IN THE HEADLINES

Affirmative Action

STILL NECESSARY OR UNFAIR ADVANTAGE?

EDUCATIONAL PUBLISHING BOOKS

THE NEW YORK TIMES EDITORIAL STAFF

Published in 2021 by New York Times Educational Publishing
in association with The Rosen Publishing Group, Inc.
29 East 21st Street, New York, NY 10010

First Edition

The New York Times
Caroline Que: Editorial Director, Book Development
Phyllis Collazo: Photo Rights/Permissions Editor
Heidi Giovine: Administrative Manager

Rosen Publishing
Megan Kellerman: Managing Editor
Brandon Battersby: Editor
Brian Garvey: Art Director

Cataloging-in-Publication Data
Names: New York Times Company.
Title: Affirmative action: still necessary or unfair advantage? / edited by the New York Times editorial staff.
Description: New York : New York Times Educational Publishing, 2021. | Series: In the headlines | Includes glossary and index.
Identifiers: ISBN 9781642823189 (library bound) | ISBN 9781642823172 (pbk.) | ISBN 9781642823196 (ebook)
Subjects: LCSH: Discrimination in employment—Government policy—United States—Juvenile literature. | Discrimination—Government policy—United States—Juvenile literature. | Civil rights—United States—History—Juvenile literature. | Affirmative action programs—United States—History—Juvenile literature.
Classification: LCC HD4903.5.U58 A337 2020 |
DDC 331.13'30973—dc23

Manufactured in the United States of America

On the cover: Charlayne Hunter, the first African-American woman admitted to the University of Georgia, leaving the registrar's office on campus after being enrolled as a student, Jan. 10, 1961; Bettmann/Getty Images.

Contents

7 Introduction

CHAPTER 1

The New Deal: The Dawn of U.S. Affirmative Action

10 Posts in Cabinets Urged for Women BY THE NEW YORK TIMES

13 Geneva Labor Body to Study Discrimination Against Employment of Aging Workers WIRELESS TO THE NEW YORK TIMES

15 Equal Job Rights for Women Asked BY THE NEW YORK TIMES

18 President Orders an Even Break for Minorities in Defense Jobs SPECIAL TO THE NEW YORK TIMES

20 New Board Set Up to End Hiring Bias SPECIAL TO THE NEW YORK TIMES

21 Warns Railroads on Negro Job Ban BY LOUIS STARK

24 Bill for Equal Pay Offered in Senate SPECIAL TO THE NEW YORK TIMES

26 Even Break Urged for All Workers SPECIAL TO THE NEW YORK TIMES

28 Wagner Act Changes BY THE NEW YORK TIMES

CHAPTER 2

Civil Rights March Affirmative Action Forward

30 Union Is Directed to Admit Negroes SPECIAL TO THE NEW YORK TIMES

32 Civil Rights Gain Reported by A.J.C. BY THE NEW YORK TIMES

34 Kennedy Statement and Executive Order on Equal Job Opportunity SPECIAL TO THE NEW YORK TIMES

48 Kennedy Sets Pattern on Civil Rights BY ANTHONY LEWIS

52 Bans on Job Bias Effective Today BY JOHN HERBERS

57 President Urges Congress to Ban All Housing Bias BY JOHN D. POMFRET

61 Senate Approves Civil Rights Bill by 71-to-20 Vote BY MARJORIE HUNTER

65 New U.S. Job Plan for Negroes Set BY ROY REED

67 Philadelphia Plan: How White House Engineered Major Victory BY ROBERT B. SEMPLE JR.

74 After Nine Years — A Homecoming for the First Black Girl at the University of Georgia BY CHARLAYNE HUNTER

CHAPTER 3

'Reverse Discrimination' Threatens Progress

93 Gains Are Made in Federal Drive for Negro Hiring BY JOHN HERBERS

100 U.S. Judge Upholds Controversial Philadelphia Plan to Increase Hiring of Minorities in Building Industry BY DONALD JANSON

103 The Stakes in Bakke BY ANTHONY LEWIS

106 N.A.A.C.P. Says Bakke Ruling Has Brought Cuts in Minority Plans BY THOMAS A. JOHNSON

109 Affirmative Action Ruling Is Called a Breakthrough BY LINDA GREENHOUSE

112 Plans to Ease Hiring Rules Attacked BY COLIN CAMPBELL

115 Rights Panel Sees Decline in U.S. Enforcement BY JULIE JOHNSON

117 Bush Vows Rights Effort on Jobs and Economic Development BY JULIE JOHNSON

121 Justices, 5 to 4, Cast Doubts on U.S. Programs That Give Preferences Based on Race BY LINDA GREENHOUSE

126 Administration Backs Affirmative Action Plan BY NEIL A. LEWIS

129 Supreme Court Dismisses Challenge in Its Main Affirmative Action Case BY LINDA GREENHOUSE

CHAPTER 4

Affirmative Action in Academia

133 Court to Weigh College Admission That Gives Minorities Preference BY LESLEY OELSNER

138 The Dangers of Racial Quotas BY LARRY M. LAVINSKY

141 Moving Beyond Affirmative Action BY THOMAS J. ESPENSHADE

145 Between the Lines of the Affirmative Action Opinion BY JOHN SCHWARTZ

149 Colleges That Ask Applicants About Brushes With the Law Draw Scrutiny BY STEPHANIE SAUL

153 Supreme Court Upholds Affirmative Action Program at University of Texas BY ADAM LIPTAK

158 'Lopping,' 'Tips' and the 'Z-List': Bias Lawsuit Explores Harvard's Admissions Secrets BY ANEMONA HARTOCOLLIS, AMY HARMON AND MITCH SMITH

168 The Rest of the Ivy League Comes to Harvard's Aid in Admissions Challenge BY ANEMONA HARTOCOLLIS

171 Justice Dept. Backs Suit Accusing Harvard of Discriminating Against Asian-American Applicants BY KATIE BENNER

176 What's at Stake in the Harvard Lawsuit? Decades of Debate Over Race in Admissions BY ANEMONA HARTOCOLLIS

181 I'm for Affirmative Action. Can You Change My Mind? BY GARY GUTTING

CHAPTER 5

The Future of Affirmative Action

185 If Affirmative Action Is Doomed, What's Next? BY DAVID LEONHARDT

191 Making Affirmative Action White Again BY IRA KATZNELSON

195 Trump Officials Reverse Obama's Policy on Affirmative Action in Schools BY ERICA L. GREEN, MATT APUZZO AND KATIE BENNER

200 The Curse of Affirmative Action BY BRET STEPHENS

204 Challengers of Affirmative Action Have a New Target: New York City's Elite High Schools BY ELIZA SHAPIRO

208 Do American Women Still Need an Equal Rights Amendment? BY SUSAN CHIRA

212 Glossary
214 Media Literacy Terms
215 Media Literacy Questions
217 Citations
222 Index

Introduction

HISTORY CAN'T BE REWRITTEN, and American history is riddled with injustices and civil inequalities. Even the Constitution wasn't originally drafted with every American in mind. But in time, the United States has taken big steps to address and rectify the harm caused by decades of discrimination against groups and individuals based on race, sex, age and other characteristics. Affirmative action is one such political device the United States has employed in efforts to accomplish this.

Affirmative action is a set of laws or policies that favor disenfranchised groups of people in efforts to make up for the discriminatory practices of the past. The term "affirmative action" first appeared in U.S. legislature in the Wagner Act of 1935, which guaranteed employees the right to organize into unions, negotiate with employers as a group and go on strike. But its applications made its first real political debut during World War II under President Franklin D. Roosevelt. To ensure that a united America was entering the great global conflict, the New Deal was proposed and included measures to promote the hiring of women into manufacturing and government positions that were predominantly held by men (now off to war) and ensure that they would be paid fair wages. Laws were also enacted to protect the rights of African-American military personnel who were fighting for their country alongside their white compatriots.

Racial equality was further accelerated during the Kennedy and Johnson administrations during the post-war and civil rights era. It was a very turbulent period for African-Americans, but the movement prompted the greatest legislative support for racial equality in work, education and civil rights that America had seen to date. Many of the government agencies created by the Kennedy administration

BETTMANN/GETTY IMAGES

From left to right: Vernon Jordan of the Urban League; Benjamin Hooks, executive director of the N.A.A.C.P. and the Rev. Jesse Jackson of PUSH (People United to Save Humanity). In a June 1978 joint news conference in New York following the U.S. Supreme Court decision in Regents of the University of California v. Bakke, Hooks called the decision "a clear-cut victory for voluntary affirmative action."

still operate today and the momentum of his proposals and the civil rights movement led to the signing of the Civil Rights Act of 1964 shortly after Kennedy's assassination.

While much progress was made during the 1960s, the next few decades would test and push the boundaries of how affirmative action would be used in private and public sectors to promote equality. During this stretch of time, the laws of the Civil Rights Act and practice of affirmative action were debated in areas such as private enterprise, unions, public works and education. Ground was both gained and lost as a result of key court cases and public policy flip-flopping.

As time ticked on into the 21st century, the debate around affirmative action evolved. Most universities managed to maintain admission policies to evade discrimination in the wake of disgruntled white college candidates. But the same policies meant to promote equality were starting to create bias toward different minority groups: Asian-Americans became the new focus of affirmative action and misuse of racial quotas.

Today, affirmative action continues to be a subject of public interest with mixed perceptions while the government is taking steps to bring us seemingly backwards: The Trump administration is set on reversing Obama-era affirmative action policies. Will affirmative action continue to be a legislative champion of equality, or have select institutions revealed how its misuse hinders the ambition of those in minority groups? Is it an antiquated practice or just one that needs to be refocused to handle today's inequality and civil rights issues?

This collection of New York Times articles chronicles some of America's greatest applications of affirmative action, including when it has made great leaps and has fallen short, how affirmative action has been received and how the perception of it has evolved over time, and where it may take equality and civil rights in the future.

CHAPTER 1

The New Deal: The Dawn of U.S. Affirmative Action

At the brink of war, President Franklin D. Roosevelt had to ensure the American people would enter World War II united and remain so both at home and on the battlefield. The country had to meet the high demands of war after having been damaged by the Great Depression. In response, F.D.R. crafted a series of economic and civil programs called the New Deal. Laws derived from it would stimulate the workforce by promoting equal job opportunities for women, who were needed to build the great American arsenal. Equally, measures would be taken to prevent discrimination among the ranks of men sent to fight the Germans and the Japanese.

Posts in Cabinets Urged for Women

BY THE NEW YORK TIMES | DEC. 4, 1936

PRESIDENT ROOSEVELT AND State Governors were urged yesterday by the National Council of Women to give "special consideration" to the appointment of women to the Cabinet and other positions of prestige and responsibility in the Federal and State Governments.

Closing a two-day session at the Hotel Astor, the council unanimously adopted a resolution declaring that women have "peculiar talents" for many government posts involving a sense of social responsibility and "respectfully" asked the President and the Governors to consider these talents in making appointments.

The council also strongly opposed any inequality of opportunity or pay between men and women in industry.

The Federal Government was "commended" in another resolution for its program providing employment for needy women and "for maintaining for women an equal wage for equal work."

APPEALS TO HOME WOMEN

Upon women themselves rests a large share of the responsibility for improving their economic status in the United States, Miss Lena Madesin Phillips, president of the International Federation of Business and Professional Women, told the conference. She asserted that women in the home owed a responsibility to womanhood in general "to see to it" that women who work for a living get adequate pay.

"A square deal for the business woman is every woman's job and the home woman should wake up to that fact," Miss Phillips said. "She can exert a powerful influence through her husband, her brother, her male friends who are the employers of labor."

Miss Jane Todd of the New York State Legislature said that the support of women for constructive legislation will go a long way toward improving government and effecting necessary social reforms. She suggested three specific measures deserving special attention from women — the Minimum Wage Law, the child labor amendment and Section 213a of the National Economy Act. The last named measure calls for dismissal of married women in any reduction of personnel in the Federal service and Miss Todd urged that women fight for its repeal.

SYMPOSIUMS ARE HELD

Leaders in the fields of education, entertainment, industry, movements for peace and the arts spoke at the symposiums at morning, afternoon and evening sessions in favor of women taking a larger role in all those fields.

Senator Joseph Clark Baldwin declared that, in recognition of the increasingly important role women are expected to play in the world of tomorrow, New York's World Fair will offer them "the greatest opportunity they have ever had" to express their ideas and their hopes.

At a radio round table in the morning, women in the audience were quick to suggest improvements in radio broadcasting at the behest of representatives of broadcasting companies. Mrs. Harold Vincent Milligan presided at the round table.

The chief criticism was directed at the "inferior" grade of music on the air, particularly in commercial programs. One woman objected vehemently to "jazz with breakfast." Music that would "soothe the nerves" was urged for the morning programs.

TEACHING OF YOUNG STRESSED

Dr. John H. Finley, speaking at a symposium on education, said that the teaching of younger children was "one of the most skilled phases of instruction," and urged extension of kindergarten and prekindergarten study. Mrs. Ellen S. Woodward, assistant administrator of the WPA, declared that women work on terms of complete equality with men in the WPA.

At a symposium on letters and the arts in the afternoon, Miss Helen Hull of Columbia University said fiction was a vital present-day force in mapping a program for better living. Dr. Howard M. LeSourd of Boston University pointed out that 85,000,000 persons view motion pictures every week and declared that any interest which claims so vast an audience deserves a place in the curriculum of schools.

The convention closed with a dinner meeting, at which speakers stressed the theme of world peace. Miss Gladys Swarthout said music in motion pictures has great potentialities for furthering international understanding and world peace. Other speakers included Mrs. Estelle M. Sternberger, executive director of World Peaceways; Mrs. Anna S. of World Peaceways; Ernest Hutcheson, dean of the Juilliard Institute of Music and Gabriel Heatter.

Geneva Labor Body to Study Discrimination Against Employment of Aging Workers

WIRELESS TO THE NEW YORK TIMES | FEB. 6, 1938

GENEVA, FEB. 5. — The study of the problem of discrimination against employing elderly workers, recently begun by the United States Department of Labor, will be extended on a world scale by the International Labor Organization, its governing body has decided on a motion of the United States workers' delegate, Robert Watt.

Mr. Watt said the problem "strikes right at the heart of a large mass of people at a period in their lives when their family responsibilities are in all probability at their highest point." He explained that American experience showed it was not hard to get protective legislation against occupational diseases but that workers paid heavily for it as they grew older through the discrimination against them on account of their age.

He asked the I. L. O. to report in October on the following questions:

"What do modern industrial processes require — young and vigorous persons capable of high-speed work? Do the new industrial processes require a more adaptable worker? Do improved hours and retirement plans cause a tendency to the employment of young people?

"Is a higher cost of workmen's compensation a factor because the older worker requires a longer period to mend? Has the older worker such family responsibilities as to make wage rates favor employment in younger age groups?"

Carter Goodrich, United States Government representative, and Henry Harriman, United States employers' representative, supported Mr. Watt. Mr. Harriman explained American employers wanted this problem solved, not only on humanitarian grounds, but to avoid increasing government relief. He said analysis "frequently shows a workman between 45 and 55, if rightly placed, is a much more valuable asset than a younger man."

The motion was not only adopted unanimously — a rare occurrence in the I. L. O., where workers, employers and governments are represented — but John Forbes-Watson, British employer delegate, who opposes nearly everything, complimented Mr. Watt on having put the case "very cleverly."

The governing body established a committee on public works. William Chalmers, Acting United States Labor Commissioner, was named chairman, and the committee was ordered to meet late in June. Speaking for the United States Government, Mr. Chalmers said he took special interest in this committee and that American experiments in tackling the depression through public works planning had been broadly successful.

The Polish Government sought to have the Bank for International Settlement included in the committee in addition to seats already provided for the League's technical organs. Leon Jouhaux, French workers' delegate, agreed it would be excellent to have the World Bank but doubted its acceptance in view of the bank's previous noncommittal attitude toward public works.

The point was shelved on Mr. Chalmers' suggestion that this and other amendments might delay the committee's getting to work.

Equal Job Rights for Women Asked

BY THE NEW YORK TIMES | MAY 22, 1938

RESOLUTIONS REFLECTING strongly feminist sympathies were adopted yesterday in the closing business session of the annual convention of the State Federation of Business and Professional Women at the Hotel Biltmore in New York. One such measure recommended to the Constitutional Convention that all laws regulating employment be based on the nature of the work, and another provided for appointment of a committee to study alleged inequalities between men and women workers in the State.

Other resolutions — all of which were adopted by unanimous vote — provided for inclusion on the active legislative program of the federation the centralization of school districts of the State; that the national federation be asked to place the Hull reciprocal trade treaties on its active legislative program; that the organization express its approval of the formation of a committee of men and women to give vocational advice to young people in their local communities; and expressed the tribute of her colleagues in the organization to Amelia Earhart.

RESOLUTION ON EMPLOYMENT

As presented to the 150 delegates, the measure asking for full employment opportunities recommended "that the principles embodied in the following provision be incorporated into the Constitution of the State of New York; 'Namely, the enjoyment of opportunities for employment in this State shall be without discrimination or preference by reason of sex, and to this end all laws regarding employment shall be based upon the nature of the work and not on the sex of the worker.'

"That a copy be sent to the Bill of Rights committee, to the committee on industry, and to all women delegates to the Constitutional Convention."

Mrs. Miriam Albee Schindler of Albany, an attorney and a member of the legislative steering committee of the National Federation, was elected president, succeeding Miss Vera McCrea.

Mrs. Schindler is a former president of the Albany Club of Business and Professional Women, vice president of the Women's Joint Legislative Forum, and legislative chairman of the City Club of Albany. She is an alumna of the Albany Law School, a member of the Albany County Bar Association and of the National Women Lawyers Association.

Other officers elected were: First vice president, Miss Esther Corwin; second vice president, Mrs. Edna Capewell; treasurer, Miss Anne Lincoln; recording secretary, Miss Alice MacChesney; corresponding secretary, Miss Helen Wurthman, and directors, Miss Frances K. Marlatt, Mrs. Matilda Hoagland, Miss Janet B. Smyth, Mrs. Julia O. Jones and Miss Louise Cheney.

BRUCE BARTON SPEAKER

Three hundred women attending the final dinner of the convention at the Biltmore last night heard Representative Bruce Barton paraphrase an old saying into his own version of the state of affairs in this country, as "the hand that wields the ladle rules the land." No denial has been made, he said, of an assertion in a Washington newspaper that $52,000,000 was expended in Kentucky to assure the re-election of Senator Alvin Barkeley.

"How many millions were ladled into Florida to make sure that the pure in heart would triumph in the renomination of Senator Pepper is not yet known," he continued, "nor how many millions will be ladled into each of the Congressional districts this Fall, where truth and the more abundant life are undertaking to defeat Republicans and — even more earnestly — to defeat those Democrats who have dared to question the bidding of the most high.

"What we need in American politics today is fewer generals and more privates in the army of voters. I would like to see the women turn their attention to the state of their local governments, to measure the

LIBRARY OF CONGRESS PRINTS AND PHOTOGRAPHS DIVISION

Representative Bruce Barton.

honesty and efficiency of administration there. Such local organizations, starting in each town, would easily and inevitably come together as larger organizations for an entire Congressional district. And when that happened, we would begin to have a real power for efficiency and economy in the halls of Congress. What we need to do is to quit thinking about Washington and begin thinking about Main Street."

Mrs. Katharine Bleecker Meigs, who presided, introduced Mrs. Sidney Borg, who sketched the phases of women's participation in the World's Fair of 1939, and Neysa McMein, artist, who predicted further advancement in feminine taste of the future on the same scale as the women of today have improved over those of a generation ago.

Dr. John I. Knudsen of the League of Nations Association reviewed the weaknesses of League negotiations among its member nations in the past.

President Orders an Even Break for Minorities in Defense Jobs

SPECIAL TO THE NEW YORK TIMES | JUNE 26, 1941

He issues an order that defense contract holders not allow discrimination against Negroes or any worker.

WASHINGTON, JUNE 25 — President Roosevelt took action today to prevent discrimination of defense jobs because of race, creed, color or national origin, asserting that "the democratic way of life within the nation can be defended successfully only with the help and support of all groups."

The President issued an executive order instructing official agencies to play their part in eliminating discrimination against Negroes and members of other minority groups and establishing a committee on fair employment practice in the Office of Production Management to deal with violations.

The Executive gave these instructions:

"All departments and agencies of the Government of the United States concerned with vocational and training programs for defense production shall take special measures appropriate to assure that such programs are administered without discrimination.

"All contracting agencies of the Government of the United States shall include in all defense contracts hereafter negotiated by them a provision obligating the contractor not to discriminate against any worker.

"There is established in the Office of Production Management a committee on fair employment practice, which shall consist of a chairman and four other members to be appointed by the President."

The order was issued principally because the government's attention had been called to cases of discrimination against Negroes in some defense industries and labor unions.

"There is evidence available that needed workers have been barred from industries engaged in defense production solely because of considerations of race, creed, color or national origin, to the detriment of workers' morale and of national unity," the President revealed. "It is the duty of employers and of labor organizations to provide for the full and equitable participation of all workers in the defense industries without discrimination."

The new unit of the OPM created to deal with the situation was instructed "to receive and investigate complaints of discrimination in violation of the provisions of this order" and to take "appropriate steps to redress grievances which it finds to be valid."

"The committee shall also recommend to the several departments and agencies of the government and to the President all measures which may be deemed necessary or proper to effectuate the provisions of this order," the President said.

New Board Set Up to End Hiring Bias

SPECIAL TO THE NEW YORK TIMES | MAY 29, 1943

WASHINGTON, MAY 28 — President Roosevelt issued an executive order today setting up a new Committee on Fair Employment Practice, with additional powers to prevent discrimination in war industry employment, and appointed Mgr. Francis J. Haas of Catholic University as chairman.

The action was designed to end widespread complaints among some groups, especially Negroes, that effective governmental action against discrimination had become impossible when the old committee was made a part of the War Manpower Commission, headed by Paul V. McNutt. Malcolm S. MacLean, president of Hampton Institute, resigned as committee chairman after Mr. McNutt ordered postponement of hearings into charges that railroads refused to employ Negroes for certain jobs.

The President has not yet appointed the new committee to serve with Mgr. Haas, but it is expected that one of its first official acts will be to reschedule the railroad hearing. Informed sources said that the committee probably would have six members, equally representative of industry and labor, in addition to the chairman.

The power given the new committee to carry out the President's policy forbidding discrimination in war industries because of race, creed, color or national origin consists of the authority to require not only war contractors but subcontractors to include a clause in their contract with the government forbidding such discrimination. The old committee could request inclusion of such a clause only in prime contracts.

Warns Railroads on Negro Job Ban

BY LOUIS STARK | DEC. 1, 1943

WASHINGTON, NOV. 30 — The President's Committee on Fair Employment Practice has notified twenty railroads and seven unions that in thirty days they must cease all discriminatory practices which result in unfair treatment of workers and job applicants because of race, creed, color or national origin.

If the roads and unions refuse to comply the cases will be turned over to President Roosevelt for enforcement of the committee's orders.

Malcolm Ross, chairman of the committee, made public today the committee's conclusions, based on testimony which showed a sharp decline in the number of Negroes employed in all but the lowest categories during the last twenty years.

Of the twenty railroads cited, ten were directed to set aside the Southeastern Agreement between them and the Brotherhood of Locomotive Firemen and Enginemen. This agreement, effective on Feb. 22, 1941, according to Mr. Ross, is a violation of Executive Order No. 9346 because it was designed to cut down the employment of Negroes as firemen and to increase the hiring of white persons in these positions.

The agreement sought to accomplish this purpose, said Mr. Ross, through setting definite percentages for white and Negro firemen; through limiting firemen's jobs to "promotable" men and then by excluding all Negro workers from promotion.

RAILROADS IN THE AGREEMENT

Roads involved in the Southeastern agreement are the Atlantic Coast Line Railway Company, Atlanta Joint Terminals, Central of Georgia Railway Company, Georgia Railroad, Jacksonville Terminal Company, Louisville and Nashville Railroad Company, Norfolk Southern Railroad Company, St. Louis-San Francisco Railway Company, Seaboard Air Line Railroad Company and the Southern Railway Company.

The other railroads involved in alleged discriminatory practices aside from the Southeastern agreement are the Baltimore & Ohio, Baltimore & Ohio Chicago Terminal, Chesapeake & Ohio, Chicago & Northwestern; Gulf, Mobile & Ohio; Illinois Central, Louisiana-Arkansas, Missouri-Kansas-Texas, Norfolk & Western and Union Pacific.

Charges filed against the Virginian Railroad were settled prior to the hearings and were withdrawn.

Final action in cases involving the Pennsylvania Railroad and New York Central have been held in abeyance pending discussions between the carriers and the committee looking toward adjustment of the complaints.

UNION NAMED BY COMMITTEE

Unions cited by the committee in its findings included The Brotherhood of Locomotive Firemen and Enginemen; Brotherhood of Railroad Trainmen; Order of Railway Conductors; Brotherhood of Railway Carmen of America; Brotherhood of Locomotive Engineers; International Association of Machinists and the International Brotherhood of Boilermakers, Iron Shipbuilders, and Helpers of America.

None of these unions appeared at the hearings held in Washington from Sept. 15 to 18, and made no official reply to the complaints lodged against them.

In citing as "unfair" the policies of these unions, the committee declared that the labor organizations were maintaining a policy which "discriminates against Negroes, because of race, in regard to membership, thus rendering it impossible (for said Negro workers) to have any adequate voice or representation with respect to grievances and the negotiation of agreements affecting working conditions, employment policy, practices and opportunities."

In each such instance, the union was notified that it must "cease and desist" from "discriminatory practices affecting the employment of Negroes."

LIBRARY OF CONGRESS PRINTS AND PHOTOGRAPHS DIVISION

A meeting of the Committee on Fair Employment Practice in July.

During the hearings, the Union Pacific Railroad, accused of discrimination against Mexicans, persons of Mexican descent, and Negroes, because of race and national origin, announced its willingness to conform to the principles of the executive orders and declared that immediate steps were being taken to investigate the specific accusations against the company. The committee has taken cognizance of this announcement and has revealed that several of the individual cases have been reported adjusted.

Testimony before the committee was that on certain roads, firing forces, which, before the last war, were 80 to 90 per cent Negro, had been reduced, by 1929, to 50 per cent or less. These reductions were accomplished, the committee declared, by continuing alteration of contracts between the unions and the roads, with each new change reducing further both the percentage of Negro workers and the type of service and the territory in which Negroes could be employed.

Bill for Equal Pay Offered in Senate

SPECIAL TO THE NEW YORK TIMES | JUNE 22, 1945

WASHINGTON, JUNE 21 — An equal pay bill to protect women war workers from wage discrimination when the war is over was introduced today by Senators Claude Pepper, Democrat, of Florida, and Wayne Morse, Republican, of Oregon. A slightly different version of the same legislation will be introduced in the House tomorrow by Representative Mary T. Norton, chairman of the Labor Committee.

The legislation provides that it would be an unfair wage practice for any employer engaged in or affecting interstate commerce to discriminate between sexes by (1) paying a different wage to a female employee for the same job, or (2) laying off a female worker and replacing her with a male employee, unless it was for a good cause or based on a non-discriminatory seniority system, or any act of Congress which requires veterans' preference.

Sponsors of the bill in the Senate explained that its administration would be along the lines of the Fair Employment Practices Committee, except that it would be administered by the Women's Bureau of the Department of Labor, whose director would be empowered to investigate complaints, hold hearings and issue rulings, interpretations and cease and desist orders. Industry committees would also be set up, as under the Fair Labor Standards Act, for industries where discriminatory wage practices are prevalent.

"These committees," the joint statement explained, "would have wide investigatory powers on wage discrimination by sex, including the right to study training and such other practices as affect a person of either sex's ability to qualify for and attain the same jobs as a member of the opposite sex. The committee could make recommendations on such things as the evaluation of job content, job classifications, standards of training and employment and appropriate wage rate ratios between job classifications."

LIBRARY OF CONGRESS PRINTS AND PHOTOGRAPHS DIVISION

Mary Anderson, head of the Women's Bureau of the Department of Labor, at her desk in June 1942.

The draft of Mrs. Norton's bill differs from the Senate bill introduced today in that it would set up a separate administrative bureau in the Department of Labor to undertake the far-reaching inspection job which she considers necessary to carry out the provisions.

The equal pay bills resulted from the urgings of a large number of women's organizations, church groups and labor groups which have become alarmed at the prospects of widespread women's unemployment and lowering of wages after the war. Miss Mary Anderson, former chief of the Women's Bureau of the Department of Labor, whose "equal pay, equal opportunities" principles were adopted by the Philadelphia Conference of the International Labor Organization, was one of those most active in the drafting of the bills.

Even Break Urged for All Workers

SPECIAL TO THE NEW YORK TIMES | SEPT. 3, 1946

Schwellenbach seeks an end of discrimination based on physical handicap.

WASHINGTON, SEPT. 2 — A plea against discrimination directed at any group of workers, particularly the physically handicapped who proved during the war that lack of limbs or eyesight does not deter them from being efficient employees, was made tonight by Lewis B. Schwellenbach, Secretary of Labor.

In an address delivered over a nation-wide radio network Mr. Schwellenbach asserted that "the value and integrity of the individual is the keystone of our democratic society," and assailed any discriminatory practices, whether they be based on sex, creed, race, religion or physical condition.

"Particularly do I wish to plead against discrimination on the basis of a physical handicap," he declared, adding that it was immaterial whether the handicap resulted from war service, industrial accident or other cause.

He said industrial management learned during the war years that the handicapped were good producers in factories and asserted it would be just as "inane" to deny a man employment because he has, say, "only one arm, as it would be to institute a policy of hiring the octopus because he has eight arms."

URGES SKILL AND TACT

"The job of breaking down discrimination is an important and a continuing one," the Secretary stated." It is inextricably bound up with the task of breaking down discrimination against groups of all kinds. The merit, or lack of merit, of a man lies not in his membership in some arbitrary group, but in the individual qualities of the man himself."

Mr. Schwellenbach asserted that "never before have so much skill and tact been required," and said that the present was no time "for stubbornness, greed, ambition or malice by individuals or groups."

He hailed labor's gains, stating that the rights to organize and bargain collectively "have become basic concepts in our democracy — hard-won rights that are here to stay."

"There are those who say that labor's motives are selfish, that the common good is not labor's aim," he said. "I know that is not true. I know that as labor achieves its basic objectives the whole nation cannot fail to prosper."

JOBS AT A RECORD HIGH

The past year saw employment "reach a record height," the Secretary noted. Including the 2,000,000 men still in the armed forces in July, "we exceeded the 60,000,000 employment goal which many economists said was fantastic."

It would be "futile," he admitted, to attempt to "minimize" the "many industrial aches and pains" that marked the reconversion period, but he declared that the Labor Department's Conciliation Commissioners were able to obtain settlement in 98 per cent of the cases in which they were called in. When they were called in before a strike actually took place they were able to bring about "peaceful agreement" in 85 per cent of the cases.

"The workers of America," he said, "now have at their service a Department of Labor that has the capacity to serve them and serve them well. ... We have an improved department and we intend to continue improving it, bringing it closer to the workers it was created for and giving them more and more effective support."

Wagner Act Changes

BY THE NEW YORK TIMES | AUG. 13, 1946

GERARD D. REILLY, retiring as a member of the three-man National Labor Relations Board after a term of five years, makes recommendations for changes in the Wagner Act that deserve a hospitable hearing both because of their prima facie reasonableness and the intimate practical experience behind them.

Mr. Reilly suggests four Wagner Act amendments. The first is clarification of the status of supervisory employees. In view of the clear statement in the text of the Wagner Act itself, defining an employer as "anyone acting in the interest of an employer," a further clarification ought not to be necessary. But the present language of the Act, and even the specific declaration of both houses of Congress against the unionization of foremen, have apparently been insufficient to prevent the majority of the NLRB from treating foremen and supervisors as employees under the Wagner Act. This amendment, therefore, has now become necessary.

The second proposal of Mr. Reilly is the withdrawal of the Act's protection from unions which strike for objectives contrary to the Act or which could be achieved by orderly processes under the Act. This amendment is also clearly desirable on its face.

The third amendment would grant to the NLRB the power to cope with unions engaged in secondary boycotts, such as the refusal recently of the Teamsters Union, AFL, and the Longshoremen and Warehousemen, CIO, to unload AFL-manned ships at Coos Bay, Ore. It might prove as difficult in practice to prevent such secondary boycotts as to prevent direct strikes; but the NLRB certainly should not be compelled to give them its direct or indirect support.

The fourth amendment suggested by Mr. Reilly is a transfer of the prosecuting and NLRB enforcement functions to the Department of Labor. This step, he argues, would make the board a fact-finding and judicial body only and increase public confidence in its impartial functions. The proposal certainly deserves study. It is, in fact, in principle not much different from the type of amendment passed by the House of Representatives in June of 1940, which separated the judicial and prosecuting functions of the board.

In addition to these proposed amendments Mr. Reilly suggests two changes which the NLRB could make in its rules of procedure without any change in the law. One would give to employers the right to petition for bargaining elections where a union claims bargaining rights and threatens to strike without resorting to NLRB procedure. Under present rules an employer can petition only if two or more unions are contesting for representation. The second change that Mr. Reilly recommends in procedure rules would accord to employers the right, co-relative with the unions, to speak freely during union-organizing campaigns, the only condition being that employers do not intimidate or discharge employees engaging in union activity. Both these changes are desirable. They are in fact desirable not only in administrative rules but in the law itself. The rights of employers in this respect should be clearly established, so that they would not fluctuate with the personnel of the Labor Board.

CHAPTER 2

Civil Rights March Affirmative Action Forward

The civil rights movement was a decades-long fight to guarantee rights to African-Americans that white Americans already enjoyed. And in the 1960s, the injustices and discrimination of America's past were met with the determination and resolve of disenfranchised African-American activists. In response, the government instituted multiple laws, agencies and commissions to promote equal rights and passed a series of civil rights acts that bestowed new protections, voting rights and educational and employment opportunities. However, as Charlayne Hunter explores in this chapter's final story, activism remained necessary to push for inclusion even after more civil rights had been secured.

Union Is Directed to Admit Negroes

SPECIAL TO THE NEW YORK TIMES | AUG. 18, 1951

Connecticut Civil Rights Board accuses it of discrimination in barring two applicants.

HARTFORD, CONN., AUG. 17 — The Connecticut Commission on Civil Rights issued an order today directing the International Brotherhood of Electrical Workers, A. F. L., Local 35, to admit two Negroes to its union membership list. The commission charged that the union discriminated against the applicants by refusing admittance to them.

Leo Parskey of Hartford, a lawyer, is chairman of a three-member tribunal that began hearings on the case in March. Under Connecticut law, the union may appeal the finding to the superior court.

The complaints against the union were brought by Mansfield T. Tilley and Warren B. Stewart, both of Hartford. More than 1,400 pages of testimony were taken during the hearings. The commission issued a finding directing that the union "cease and desist from excluding" the complainants from "full membership because of race."

"The history of the union shows a pattern of discrimination against Negroes," the finding said. "No Negroes have ever been admitted into the union. The union admits that the complainants were excluded but claims that their exclusion was justified. It contends that the complainants did not meet the eligibility requirements established by the local union for their admission as apprentices, first, because they were too old, second, because they were not sponsored by an employer."

The tribunal rejected the claims of the union.

"The union has given preference to sons and other relatives of members," it added. "The inbreeding which such nepotism nurtures may discriminate against some white persons but Negroes are thereby excluded from membership absolutely. The evil created by arbitrary admissions practices is that they permit the very discrimination which the act seeks to prevent."

The finding went on to say that "the union did not act" on the applications of the two Negroes "nor did it inform the complainants of its failure to act."

"On two occasions other than those concerning the complainants the union had an opportunity to admit Negroes to its membership," the finding said. "On each such occasion the union declined to do so."

Civil Rights Gain Reported by A.J.C.

BY THE NEW YORK TIMES | AUG. 5, 1959

Study shows legislatures of states are moving to end discrimination.

A SURVEY OF civil rights laws enacted in 1958-59 presents "striking evidence" that state legislatures are moving to wipe out racial and religious discrimination, the American Jewish Congress said yesterday.

A study by the Congress shows that twenty-four laws dealing with discrimination were passed by fourteen states this year. Both in number and content, the study notes, the civil rights laws enacted by the states this year equaled and may exceed those of any year in the last decade.

In all likelihood, it was explained, the record will be surpassed. Leo Pfeffer, director of the group's commission on law and social action, said the record depended on legislative action in Pennsylvania on a bill prohibiting discrimination in education.

The bill has passed the House and now awaits Senate action.

The study summarized the principal legislative advances of 1959 as follows:

• California and Ohio adopted enforceable fair-employment laws. This raised to sixteen the number of states with such legislation.

• The first state laws against discrimination in the general housing market were adopted. Theretofore, all state laws on housing were confined to accommodations receiving some form of governmental aid. This year, Colorado, Connecticut, Massachusetts and Oregon adopted broad fair-housing legislation, following New York City and Pittsburgh.

• Maine became the twenty-fourth state to enact an enforceable law prohibiting discrimination in places of public accommodation. California, Connecticut, Kansas and Wisconsin improved the effectiveness of their laws in this area.

• California, Connecticut, Missouri, New Mexico and Ohio passed laws relating to discrimination in employment on the basis of race, color, religion, national origin or ancestry.

• Washington adopted legislation making it an unfair practice to require any person applying for financial credit to state his religion, race or national origin. Missouri enacted a bill giving permanent status to a commission on human rights that was created last year as a temporary agency.

• California, Idaho and Nevada repealed their ban on marriages between whites and non-whites. The Oregon Legislature ratified the Fifteenth Amendment to the United States Constitution and the California Legislature ratified the Fourteenth Amendment.

The Fifteenth Amendment provides for equal rights for white and non-white citizens. The Fourteenth Amendment guarantees that citizenship rights shall not be abridged.

Kennedy Statement and Executive Order on Equal Job Opportunity

SPECIAL TO THE NEW YORK TIMES | MARCH 7, 1961

WASHINGTON, MARCH 6 — *Following are President Kennedy's statement and the text of an order he issued today on equal employment opportunity:*

PRESIDENT'S STATEMENT

I am today issuing an Executive order combining the President's Committee on Government Contracts and the President's Committee on Government Employment policy into a single President's Committee on Equal Employment Opportunity.

Through this vastly strengthened machinery I intend to insure that Americans of all colors and beliefs will have equal access to employment within the Government, and with those who do business with the Government.

The implementation of this policy has been hampered by lack of personnel, by inadequate procedures and ineffective enforcement. As a result Americans who are members of minority groups have often been unjustly denied the opportunity to work for the Government or for Government contractors.

This order provides for centralization of responsibility for these policies under the Vice President. It requires the Secretary of Labor — with all the resources of the Department of Labor at his command — to supervise the implementation of equal employment policies. And it grants, in specific terms, sanctions sweeping enough to ensure compliance.

In this order, I am also directing a complete study of current Government employment practices — an examination of the status of members of minority groups in every department, agency and office of the Federal Government. When this survey — the most thorough ever undertaken — is completed we will have an accurate assessment of our present position and a yardstick by which to measure future progress.

I have dedicated my Administration to the cause of equal opportunity in employment by the Government or its contractors. The Vice President, the Secretary of Labor and the other members of this committee share my dedication. I have no doubt that the vigorous enforcement of this order will mean the end of such discrimination.

In this connection I have already directed all departments to take immediate action to broaden the Government employment opportunities for members of minority groups.

EXECUTIVE ORDER

Whereas, discrimination because of race, creed, color or national origin is contrary to the constitutional principles and policies of the United States; and

Whereas, it is the plain and positive obligation of the United States Government to promote and ensure equal opportunity for all qualified persons, without regard to race, creed, color or national origin, employed or seeking employment with the Federal Government and on Government contracts; and

Whereas, it is the policy of the executive branch of the Government to encourage by positive measures equal opportunity for all qualified persons within the government; and

Whereas, it is the general interest and welfare of the United States to promote its economy, security and national defense through the most efficient and effective utilization of all available manpower; and

Whereas, a review and analysis of existing executive orders, practices and Government agency procedures relating to Government employment and compliance with existing non-discrimination contract provisions reveal an urgent need for expansion and strengthening of efforts to promote full equality of employment opportunity; and

Whereas, a single Governmental committee should be charged with responsibility for accomplishing these objectives:

Now, therefore, by virtue of the authority vested in me as President of the United States by the Constitution and statutes of the United States, it is ordered as follows:

PART I — ESTABLISHMENT OF THE PRESIDENT'S COMMITTEE ON EQUAL EMPLOYMENT OPPORTUNITY

SECTION 101. There is hereby established the President's Committee on Equal Employment opportunity.

SECTION 102. The committee shall be composed as follows:

(A) The Vice President of the United States, who is hereby designated chairman of the committee and who shall preside at meetings of the committee.

(B) The Secretary of Labor, who is hereby designated vice chairman of the committee and who shall act as chairman in the absence of the chairman. The vice chairman shall have general supervision and direction of the work of the committee and of the execution and implementation of the policies and purposes of this order.

(C) The chairman of the Atomic Energy Commission, the Secretary of Commerce, the Attorney General, the Secretary of Defense, the Secretaries of the Army, Navy and Air Force, the Administrator of General Services, the Chairman of the Civil Service Commission, and the Administrator of National Aeronautics and Space Administration. Each such member may designate an alternate to represent him in his absence.

(D) Such other members as the President may from time to time appoint.

(E) An executive vice chairman, designated by the President, who shall be ex officio a member of the committee. The executive vice chairman shall assist the chairman, the vice chairman and the committee. Between meetings of the committee he shall be primarily responsible for carrying out the functions of the committee and may act for the committee pursuant to its rules, delegations and other directives. Final action in individual cases or classes of cases may be taken and final orders may be entered on behalf of the committee by the executive vice chairman when the committee so authorizes.

SECTION 103. The committee shall meet upon the call of the chairman and at such other times as may be provided by its rules and regulations. It shall (a) consider and adopt rules and regulations to govern its proceedings; (b) provide generally for the procedure and policies to implement this; (c) consider reports as to progress under this order; (d) consider and act, where necessary or appropriate, upon matters which may be presented to it by any of its members; and (e) make such reports to the President as he may require or the committee shall deem appropriate. Such reports shall be made at least once annually and shall include specific references to the actions taken and results achieved by each department and agency. The chairman may appoint sub-committees to make special studies on a continuing basis.

PART II — NONDISCRIMINATION IN GOVERNMENT EMPLOYMENT

SECTION 201. The President's Committee on Equal Employment Opportunity, established by this order, is directed immediately to scrutinize and study employment practices of the Government of the United States, and to consider and recommend additional affirmative steps which should be taken by executive departments and agencies to realize more fully the national policy of nondiscrimination within the executive branch of the Government.

SECTION 202. All executive departments and agencies are directed to initiate forthwith studies of current Government employment practices within their responsibility. The studies shall be in such form as the committee may prescribe and shall include statistics on current employment patterns, a review of current procedures, and the recommendation of positive measures for the elimination of any discrimination, direct or indirect, which now exists. Reports and recommendations shall be submitted to the executive vice chairman of the committee no later than sixty days from the effective date of this order, and the committee, after considering such reports and recommendations, shall report to the President on the current situation and recommend positive measures to accomplish the objectives of this order.

SECTION 203. The policy expressed in Executive Order No. 10590 of Jan. 18, 1955 (20 F. R. 409), with respect to the exclusion and prohibition of discrimination against any employee or applicant for employment in the Federal Government because of race, color, religion or national origin, is hereby reaffirmed.

SECTION 204. The President's Committee on Government Employment Policy established by Executive Order No. 10590 on Jan. 18, 1955 (20 F. R. 409), as amended by Executive Order No. 10722 of Aug. 5, 1957 (22 F. R. 6287), is hereby abolished, and the powers, functions and duties of that committee are hereby transferred to, and henceforth shall be vested in, and exercised by, the President's Committee on Equal Employment Opportunity in addition to the powers conferred by this order.

PART III — OBLIGATIONS OF GOVERNMENT CONTRACTORS AND SUBCONTRACTORS

SUBPART A — CONTRACTORS' AGREEMENTS

SECTION 301. Except in contracts exempted in accordance with Section 303 of this order, all Government contracting agencies shall include in every Government contract hereafter entered into the following provisions:

"In connection with the performance of work under this contract, the contractor agrees as follows:

"(1) The contractor will not discriminate against any employee or applicant for employment because of race, creed, color or national origin. The contractor will take affirmative action to ensure that applicants are employed, and that employees are treated during employment, without regard to their race, creed, color or national origin. Such action shall include, but not be limited to, the following: employment, upgrading, demotion or transfer; recruitment or recruitment advertising; layoff or termination; rates of pay or other forms of compensation; and selection for training, including apprenticeship. The contractor agrees to post in conspicuous places, available to employees and applicants for employment notices to be provided by the contracting officer setting forth the provisions of this nondiscrimination clause.

"(2) The contractor will, in all solicitations or advertisements for employees placed by or on behalf of the contractor, state that all qualified applicants will receive consideration for employment without regard to race, creed, color or national origin.

"(3) The contractor will send to each labor union or representative of workers with which he has a collective bargaining agreement or other contract or understanding, a notice, to be provided by the agency contracting officer, advising the said labor union or worker's representative of the contractor's commitments under this section, and shall post copies of the notice in conspicuous places available to employees and applicants for employment.

"(4) The contractor will comply with all provisions of Executive Order No. 10925 of March 6, 1961, and of the rules, regulations and relevant orders of the President's Committee on Equal Employment Opportunity, created thereby.

"(5) The contractor will furnish all information and reports, required, by Executive Order No. 10925 of March 6, 1961, and by the rules, regulations and orders of the said committee, or pursuant thereto, and will permit access to his books, records and accounts by the contracting agency and the committee for purposes of investigation to ascertain compliance with such rules, regulations and orders.

"(6) In the event of the contractor's non-compliance with the nondiscrimination clauses of this contract or with any of the said rules, regulations or orders, this contract may be canceled in whole or in part and the contractor may be declared ineligible for further Government contracts in accordance with procedures authorized in Executive Order No. 10925 of March 6, 1961, and such other sanctions may be imposed and remedies invoked as provided in the said executive order or by rule, regulation or order of the President's Committee on Equal Employment Opportunity, or as otherwise provided by law.

"(7) The contractor will include the provisions of the foregoing paragraphs (1) through (6) in every subcontract or purchase order unless exempted by rules, regulations or orders of the President's Committee on Equal Employment Opportunity issued pursuant to Section 303 of Executive Order No. 10925 of March 6, 1961, so that such provisions will be binding upon each subcontractor or vendor. The contractor will take such action with respect to any subcontract or purchase order as the contracting agency may direct as a means of enforcing such provisions, including sanctions for noncompliance: provided, however, that in the event the contractor becomes involved in, or is threatened with, litigation with a subcontractor or vendor as a result of such direction by the contracting agency, the contractor may request the United States to enter into such litigation to protect the interests of the United States."

SECTION 302. (A) Each contractor having a contract containing the provisions prescribed in Section 301 shall file, and shall cause each of its subcontractors to file, compliance reports with the contracting agency, which will be subject to review by the committee upon its request. Compliance reports shall be filed within such times and shall contain such information as to the practices, policies, programs and employment statistics of the contractor and each subcontractor, and shall be in such form, as the committee may prescribe.

(B) Bidders or prospective contractors or subcontractors may be required to state whether they have participated in any previous contract subject to the provisions of this order, and in that event to submit, on behalf of themselves and their proposed subcontractors, compliance reports prior to or as an initial part of their bid or negotiation of a contract.

(C) Whenever the contractor or subcontractor has a collective bargaining agreement or other contract or understanding with a labor union or other representative of workers, the compliance report shall include such information as to the labor union's or other representative's practices and policies affecting compliance as the committee may prescribe: provided, that to the extent such information is within the exclusive possession of a labor union or other workers' representative and the labor union or representative shall refuse to furnish such information to the contractor, the contractor shall so certify to the contracting agency as part of its compliance report and shall set forth what efforts he has made to obtain such information.

(D) The committee may direct that any bidder or prospective contractor or subcontractor shall submit, as part of his compliance report, a statement in writing, signed by an authorized officer or agent of any labor union or other workers' representative with which the bidder or prospective contractor deals, together with supporting information, to the effect that the said labor union's or representative's practices and policies do not discriminate on the grounds of race, color, creed or national origin, and that the labor union or representative either will affirmatively cooperate, within the limits of his legal and contractual authority, in the implementation of the policy and provisions of this order or that it consents and agrees that recruitment, employment and the terms and conditions of employment under the proposed contract shall be in accordance with the purposes and provisions of the order. In the event that the union or representative shall refuse to execute such a statement, the compliance report shall so certify and set forth what efforts have been made to secure such a statement.

SECTION 303. The committee may, when it deems that special circumstances in the national interest so require, exempt a contracting agency from the requirement of including the provisions of Section 301 of this order in any specific contract, subcontract or purchase order. The committee may, by rule or regulation, also exempt certain classes of contracts, subcontracts or purchase order (A) where work is to be or has been performed outside the United States and no recruitment of workers within the limits of the United States is involved; (B) for standard commercial supplies or raw materials; or (C) involving less than specified amounts of money or specified numbers of workers.

SUBPART B — LABOR UNIONS AND REPRESENTATIVES OF WORKERS

SECTION 304. The committee shall use its best efforts, directly and through contracting agencies, contractors, state and local officials and public and private agencies, and all other available instrumentalities, to cause any labor union, recruiting agency or other representative of workers who is or may be engaged in work under Government contracts to comply in the implementation of, the purposes of this order.

SECTION 305. The committee may, to effectuate the purposes of Section 304 of this order, hold hearings, public or private, with respect to the practices and policies of any such labor organization. It shall from time to time submit special reports to the President concerning discriminatory practices and policies of any such labor organization, and may recommend remedial action, if in its judgment, such action is necessary or appropriate. It may also notify any Federal, state or local agency of its conclusions and recommendations with respect to any such labor organization which in its judgment has failed to cooperate with the committee, contracting agencies, contractors or subcontractors in carrying out the purposes of this order.

SUBPART C — POWERS AND DUTIES OF THE PRESIDENT'S COMMITTEE ON EQUAL EMPLOYMENT OPPORTUNITY AND OF CONTRACTING AGENCIES

SECTION 306. The committee shall adopt such rules and regulations and issue such orders as it deems necessary and appropriate to achieve the purposes of this order, including the purposes of Part II hereof relating to discrimination in Government employment.

SECTION 307. Each contracting agency shall be primarily responsible for obtaining compliance with the rules, regulations and orders of the committee with respect to contracts entered into by such agency or its contractors, or affecting its own employment practices. All contracting agencies shall comply with the committee's rules in discharging their primary responsibility for securing compliance with the provisions of contracts and otherwise with the terms of this executive order and of the rules, regulations and orders of the committee pursuant hereto. They are directed to cooperate with the committee, and to furnish the committee such information and assistance as it may require in the performance of its functions under this order. They are further directed to appoint or designate, from among the agency's personnel, compliance officers. It shall be the duty of such officers to seek compliance with the objectives of this order by conference, conciliation, mediation or persuasion.

SECTION 308. The committee is authorized to delegate to any officer, agency or employee in the executive branch of the Government any function of the committee under this order, except the authority to promulgate rules and regulations of a general nature.

SECTION 309. (A) The committee may itself investigate the employment practices of any Government contractor or subcontractor, or initiate such investigation by the appropriate contracting agency or through the Secretary of Labor, to determine whether or not the contractual provisions specified in Section 301 of this order have been violated. Such investigation shall be conducted in accordance with the procedures established by the committee, and the investigating agency shall report to the committee any action taken or recommended.

(B) The committee may receive and cause to be investigated complaints by employees or prospective employees of a Government contractor or subcontractor which allege discrimination contrary to the contractual provisions specified in Section 301 of this order. The appropriate contracting agency or the Secretary of Labor, as the case may be, shall report to the committee what action has been taken or is recommended with regard to such complaints.

SECTION 310. (A) The committee, or any agency or officer of the United States designated by rule, regulation or order of the committee, may hold such hearings, public or private, as the committee may deem advisable for compliance, enforcement or educational purposes.

(B) The committee may hold, or cause to be held, hearings in accordance with section (A) of this section prior to imposing, ordering or recommending the imposition of penalties and sanctions under this order, except that no order for debarment of any contractor from further Government contracts shall be made without a hearing.

SECTION 311. The committee shall encourage the furtherance of an educational program by employer, labor, civic, educational, religious and other nongovernmental groups in order to eliminate or reduce the basic causes of discrimination in employment on the ground of race, creed, color or national origin.

SUBPART D — SANCTIONS AND PENALTIES

SECTION 312. In accordance with such rules, regulations or orders as the committee may issue or adopt, the committee or the appropriate contracting agency may:

(A) Publish, or cause to be published, the names of contractors or unions which it has concluded have complied or have failed to comply with the provisions of this order of the rules, regulations and orders of the committee.

(B) Recommend to the Department of Justice that, in cases where there is substantial or material violation or the threat of substantial or material violation of the contractual provisions set forth in Section 301 of this order, appropriate proceedings be brought to enforce those provisions, including the enjoining, within the limitations of applicable law, or organizations, individuals or groups who prevent or directly or indirectly, or seek to prevent directly or indirectly, compliance with the aforesaid provisions.

(C) Recommend to the Department of Justice that criminal proceedings be brought for the furnishing of false information to any contracting agency or to the committee as the case may be.

(D) Terminate, or cause to be terminated, any contract, or any portion or portions thereof, for failure of the contractor or subcontractor to comply with the nondiscrimination provisions of the contract. Contracts may be terminated absolutely or continuance of contracts may be conditioned upon a program for future compliance approved by the contracting agency.

(E) Provide that any contracting agency shall refrain from entering into further contracts, or extensions or other modifications of existing contracts, with any non-complying contractor, until such contractor has satisfied the committee that he has established and will carry out personnel and employment policies in compliance with the provisions of this order.

(F) Under rules and regulations prescribed by the committee, each contracting agency shall make reasonable efforts within a reasonable time limitation to secure compliance with the contract provisions of this order by methods of conference, conciliation, mediation, and persuasion before proceedings shall be instituted under Paragraph (B) of this section, or before a contract shall be terminated in whole or in part under Paragraph (D) of this section for failure of a contractor or subcontractor to comply with the contract provisions of this order.

SECTION 313. Any contracting agency taking any action authorized by this section, whether on its own motion, or as directed by the committee, or under the committee's rules and regulations, shall promptly notify the committee of such action or reasons for not acting. Where the committee itself makes a determination under this section, it shall promptly notify the appropriate contracting agency of the action recommended. The agency shall take such action and shall report the results thereof to the committee within such time as the committee shall provide.

SECTION 314. If the committee shall so direct, contracting agencies shall not enter into contracts with any bidder or prospective contractor unless the bidder or prospective contractor has satisfactorily complied with the provisions of this order or submits a program for compliance acceptable to the committee or, if the committee so authorizes, to the contracting agency.

SECTION 315. Whenever a contracting agency terminates a contract, or whenever a contractor has been debarred from further Government contracts, because of noncompliance with the contractor provisions with regard to nondiscrimination, the committee, or the contracting agency involved, shall promptly notify the Controller General of the United States.

SUBPART E — CERTIFICATES OF MERIT

SECTION 316. The committee may provide for issuance of a United States Government certificate of merit to employers or employee organizations which are or may hereafter be engaged in work under Government contracts, if the committee is satisfied that the personnel and employment practices of the employer, or that the personnel, training, apprenticeship, membership, grievance and representation, upgrading and other practices and policies of the employee organization, conform to the purposes and provisions of this order.

SECTION 317. Any certificate of merit may at any time be suspended or revoked by the committee if the holder thereof, in the judgment of the committee, has failed to comply with the provisions of this order.

SECTION 318. The committee may provide for the exemption of any employer or employee organization from any requirement for furnishing information as to compliance if such employer or employee organization has been awarded a certificate of merit which has not been suspended or revoked.

PART IV — MISCELLANEOUS

SECTION 401. Each contracting agency (except the Department of Justice) shall defray such necessary expenses of the committee as may be authorized by law, including Section 214 of the Act of May 3, 1945, 59 Stat. 134 (31 U. S. C. 691): provided, that no agency shall supply more than 50 per cent of the funds necessary to carry out the purposes of this order. The Department of Labor shall provide necessary space and facilities for the committee. In the case of the

Department of Justice, the contribution shall be limited to furnishing legal services.

SECTION 402. This order shall become effective thirty days after its execution. The General Services Administration shall take appropriate action to revise the standard Government contract forms to accord with the provisions of this order and of the rules and regulations of the committee.

SECTION 403. Executive Order No. 10479 of Aug. 13, 1953 (18 F. R. 4899), together with Executive Orders No. 10482 of Aug. 15, 1953 (18 F. R. 4944) and 10733 of Oct. 10, 1957 (22 F. R. 8135), amending that order, and Executive Order No. 10557 of Sept. 3, 1954 (19 F. R. 5655), are hereby revoked and the Government contract committee established by Executive Order No. 10479 is abolished. All records and property of or in the custody of the said committee are hereby transferred to the President's Committee on Equal Employment Opportunity, which shall wind up the outstanding affairs of the Government Contract Committee.

JOHN F. KENNEDY.
The White House,
March 6, 1961.

Kennedy Sets Pattern on Civil Rights

BY ANTHONY LEWIS | MARCH 12, 1961

President moves through his executive powers rather than risk losing battle in Congress.

WASHINGTON, MARCH 11 — The outlines of President Kennedy's initial approach to the problem of Negro rights became clear this week with the issuance of his executive order on equal job opportunities.

Two characteristics stand out in that approach. The President is relying for the moment on executive action, with no calls for new civil rights legislation. And he's putting his emphasis on measures to help the Negro economically.

The reliance on executive power is no surprise. Well before Mr. Kennedy's inauguration it was the general political judgment here that pressing for new civil rights legislation at the very beginning of a new Administration would be damaging in other fields and produce nothing on civil rights.

The economic emphasis results from a long-established fact — that minority groups suffer worst in a recession. The old saying is that Negroes are the last hired and the first fired. The proportion of Negroes now unemployed is twice the figure for whites.

Thus the general anti-recession measures sent to Congress by Mr. Kennedy are regarded in the White House as of special importance to Negroes and other minority groups.

LONG-TERM PROPOSALS

In the same way the long-term welfare proposals of the administration can be regarded as notably helpful to minorities.

The Executive order issued last Monday was a specific move for Negro economic advancement. Its purpose was to put some teeth into the long-standing (but often largely theoretical) policy against discrimination in hiring by the Government or its contractors.

ABBIE ROWE/PHOTOQUEST/GETTY IMAGES

President Kennedy speaking at the State Department in Washington, D.C., earlier this month.

The order went about as far as words could go to stiffen the policy. It was broad in its coverage, strong in its language and sweeping in the enforcement powers it established.

A new committee headed by Vice President Johnson will police both Government and contractor employment, handled previously by separate groups set up by former President Eisenhower. The Labor Department, with its large staff, will be the chief investigative and enforcement arm of the committee, and Secretary of Labor Arthur Goldberg will serve as vice chairman.

Under the order, all contractors and subcontractors on Government jobs will have to file regular compliance reports, open their books and records to the committee and affirmatively recruit employees without regard to race. Failure to obey committee directives may lead to cancellation of contracts and even to the barring of offending contractors from future bids on Government jobs.

There is also an attempt to get at some labor unions' exclusion of Negroes from membership. The order directs the new committee to counsel with unions that discriminate, publicize them and to hold public hearings for enforcement or "educational" purposes.

Without waiting for the executive order, the President had taken steps to increase Negro employment in government.

He has named a number of Negroes to top-level jobs — housing administrator, an ambassador, two White House aides and others. He has directed all departments to see that qualified Negroes are hired at all levels.

'MORAL AUTHORITY'

Outside the economic area, Mr. Kennedy has made a start on using what he termed during the campaign the President's "moral authority." He has spoken out on behalf of those seeking to implement school desegregation in the face of local opposition.

His brother, Robert, the Attorney General, has been doing a great deal on civil rights — most of it unpublicized. It became known that he had telephoned lawyers and political leaders in Louisiana to try to get them to call off their war against desegregation in New Orleans. It is not generally known that he has called Governors and other leaders in almost every other state of the South, for such purposes as obtaining voting records and getting the bail on a Negro demonstrator lowered.

REAL EFFORT

How hard will the administration push along these lines it has so far laid out?

Every indication is that there will be a real effort. Secretary Goldberg has men touring all the Negro colleges in the country looking for potential government employees. Robert Kennedy will surely go on trying to persuade Southern politicians.

But, of course, there will be strong demands for more action, in other fields. The Republicans in Congress have begun sniping at the

Administration for not presenting one, though President Eisenhower waited three years before producing his first civil rights message. Some Negro leaders have demanded immediate legislative action, but there is reason to believe that most are prepared to go along with the President on some delay.

At this point the only other major civil rights action that seems likely to come from the Administration in the immediate future is a fresh Justice Department attack on the blocking of Negro voting in the South. As soon as the department's new hierarchy can get gears meshed, investigations and suits under the 1957 Civil Rights Act will begin.

The President himself made clear at this week's news conference that there would be no early demand for legislation. He said he would recommend new laws "when I feel that there's necessity for Congressional action with a chance of getting that Congressional action."

HOUSING QUESTION

Nor does it seem likely that further large-scale executive orders will be forthcoming soon. This includes the much-debated idea of an order conditioning the use of Federal funds for housing on a pledge that the housing will be open to all regardless of race.

Politics is the most urgent reason for holding off such broad-scale moves as a housing order or a legislative program on civil rights. The President needs every Southern vote he can get in Congress for his economic and social program, and he believes it would be foolish to alienate any of those votes at this time.

Administration officials insist that the continuing good relations with the South do not indicate any weakness in the President's civil rights stand. They argue that his steps so far, though perhaps not greatly dramatized, amount to much more action on behalf of Negro rights than any President could claim after less than two months in office.

Bans on Job Bias Effective Today

BY JOHN HERBERS | JULY 2, 1965

WASHINGTON, JULY 1 — The first national law prohibiting discrimination against minority groups in private employment goes into effect tomorrow.

The prohibition, contained in Title VII of the Civil Rights Act of 1964, has the potential of opening vast new employment opportunities for Negroes, other racial groups, religious minorities and women.

The extent and time of its effectiveness, however, are in doubt for several reasons. Chief among these is the fact that the law is cumbersome, possibly riddled with loopholes, and gives the agency administering it, the Equal Employment Opportunity Commission, no enforcement powers.

Also, President Johnson waited so long to appoint the commission — until May 10 — that it cannot be in full operation for several months. It now has only a skeleton staff operating out of temporary offices and has yet to formulate its policies.

BUSINESSMEN CONCERNED

One provision that attracted little attention when the law was passed — the ban against discrimination for reasons of sex — has recently caused a stir in the business community because no one knows to what extent women will want to move into jobs traditionally held by men, or vice versa.

Further complicating the situation has been the fact that the chairman of the commission, Franklin D. Roosevelt Jr., has been giving much of his attention to politics in New York where he was considered a potential candidate for Mayor. Mr. Roosevelt announced at a news conference here today that he would not make the race.

That out of the way, Mr. Roosevelt said the commission will be "in business tomorrow morning," will welcome complaints and inquiries and will soon begin formulating guidelines to help businessmen and job hunters know what to expect of the commission.

Title VII is one major provision of the Civil Rights Act, which was signed by President Johnson last July 2. Congress delayed the effective date of Title VII for one year to give all concerned time for orderly compliance and to enable the commission to be appointed and begin functioning.

The enactment of Title VII culminated two decades of effort by civil rights advocates to make fair employment practices a statutory requirement. In 1941, President Roosevelt, father of the commission's chairman, established by executive order a Fair Employment Practices Commission. He acted after Negroes had threatened to march on Washington to protest discrimination in defense jobs.

That F.E.P.C. died in 1946. Since then the Government has had a series of agencies at work to prevent discrimination in connection with Government contracts. But it was not until the civil rights breakthrough of 1964 that the Government attempted to forbid employment discrimination throughout the entire economy.

Title VII forbids discrimination in hiring, dismissal, promotion or any other term or condition of employment on the basis of race, color, religion, sex or national origin on the part of employers, unions and employment agencies.

For the first year, until July 2, 1966, the law applies to employers and unions with 100 or more workers or members; the second year, 75 or more; the third year, 50 or more; and thereafter, 25 or more.

There are a number of exemptions in the law. These include cases in which religion, sex or national origin is a genuine occupational qualification necessary to the operation of a business or school. Discrimination against Communists is permitted.

RACIAL BALANCE NOT NEEDED

Reverse discrimination is outlawed. That is, an employer is not required to maintain racial balance in his place of business. On the other hand, a business operating on or near an Indian reservation may give preference to Indians. Existing preference laws for veterans remain in effect.

Discrimination is not defined in the law and lawyers concerned with it say this will be done over a period of time through the commission and the courts.

Any individual or a member of the commission may file a complaint. If the complainant lives in one of 27 states that have a fair employment practices law he must act first under the state law and wait 60 days to begin action under the Federal commission.

If the commission finds discrimination exists it must try to end it by conciliation. If conciliation fails, the complainant may bring a civil suit in a Federal District Court, which may appoint an attorney for him and permit him to proceed without cost.

The Attorney General may intervene for a complainant if he considers the case of general public importance — a pattern of discrimination, for instance.

Mr. Roosevelt appeared before a Senate Appropriations subcommittee today and said the commission would stress conciliation.

"We have no intention to persecute or interfere with the rightful prerogatives of any employer, labor union, or employment agency," he said.

He requested $3.2 million to run the agency its first year. He said a staff of 190 was foreseen. Regional offices will be established by the end of the year in New York, Los Angeles, Chicago, Cleveland, Dallas and Atlanta.

HOPES TO SET RULES SOON

At a news conference later, Mr. Roosevelt said the commission was "working on some substantive regulations and hopes to have them in the next few weeks."

He indicated, however, that the nature and amount of complaints would guide policy.

"It's hard to tell what the problems will be until we see the kind of complaints we get," he said.

All complaints, he said, must be based on actions occurring after July 1.

Administration sources said President Johnson had waited 10 months to appoint the commission because he had been preoccupied with other matters and because he had wanted a widely known person to serve as chairman.

On May 10, the President announced he had appointed Mr. Roosevelt, then Under Secretary of Commerce, as chairman, and the following members:

Mrs. Eileen Hernandez, assistant chief of the California Fair Employment Practices Division; Richard Graham, Peace Corps director in Tunisia; the Rev. Luther Holcomb of Dallas; and Samuel C. Jackson, a lawyer for the state of Kansas.

Since their appointment the commissioners have been spending much of their time making talks to business groups and civil rights groups in an effort to prepare the country for compliance.

Although the commission will be concerned primarily with racial discrimination, the word "sex," which was inserted in the law — some said with tongue in cheek — by Representative Howard W. Smith, Democrat of Virginia, is expected to create some problems for the agency.

"What about sex?" Mr. Roosevelt was asked at the news conference.

"Don't get me started," Mr. Roosevelt replied with a laugh. "I'm all for it."

"Seriously," he added, "we can't foretell what problems there will be in this area. We will have to learn as we go along."

So far, there has been no organized effort by women's groups to use the law to remove barriers against females in certain job classifications.

Businessmen, however, have imagined many kinds of possibilities, such as women applying for jobs as truck drivers and men applying to be clerks in a women's clothing store.

Newspapers and advertisers have been concerned about whether they can continue to publish classified ads designating the sex of help wanted.

President Urges Congress to Ban All Housing Bias

BY JOHN D. POMFRET | APRIL 29, 1966

WASHINGTON, APRIL 28 — President Johnson asked Congress today to enact "the first effective Federal law against discrimination" on racial or religious grounds in the sale and rental of all housing.

Present Federal strictures on housing discrimination apply only to buildings whose mortgages are insured by the Federal Housing Administration or the Veterans Administration under an executive order issued by President Kennedy in 1962.

Today's request was included in the President's Civil Rights Message. It is expected to arouse more controversy and opposition in Congress than the other provisions proposed by Mr. Johnson in the message.

MAIN IMPACT IN SOUTH

The other provisions, like most past civil rights legislation, would have their principal impact in the Southern states. Discrimination in housing, however, is widely practiced in all parts of the country and many Congressmen from the North as well as the South will be under pressure from constituents who want Negroes to continue to be excluded from their neighborhoods.

Mr. Johnson also proposed a far stronger law than anything now on the statute books to protect Negroes and others who work for racial justice from interference in the exercise of their rights.

He sought legislation to insure that Federal and state court juries are selected in nondiscriminatory fashion.

The President also asked Congress to broaden the Attorney General's authority to bring suit for the desegregation of schools and public facilities.

MORE F.B.I. AGENTS SOUGHT

He asked the Senate to approve legislation that cleared the House yesterday to give enforcement powers to the Equal Employment Opportunity Commission, the agency established by the Civil Rights Act of 1964.

Lastly, he asked Congress to provide funds for 100 more agents for the Federal Bureau of Investigation in order to strengthen the bureau's capacity to deal with civil rights crimes.

The bureau has 6,492 agents. Mr. Johnson said in his message that at times in the recent past as many as a third of them had been assigned to the investigation of civil rights matters.

Shortly before he sent his proposals to Capitol Hill, Mr. Johnson discussed them with a group of civil rights leaders at the White House.

Attorney General Nicholas deB. Katzenbach, who participated in the meeting, described the reaction of the civil rights leaders as "extremely warm."

One of the civil rights proponents said that the group regarded Mr. Johnson's proposals favorably, but probably would try to strengthen them.

He said that the group would probably try to get Congress to enact legislation to transfer state criminal trials to Federal courts in areas with "segregated systems of justice."

He said that the civil rights advocates might also attempt to secure passage of legislation to pay Federal indemnities to civil rights workers injured while attempting to secure rights for Negroes.

NOT DISAPPOINTED

He emphasized that the civil rights leaders who met with the President were in no way disappointed with Mr. Johnson's proposals and intended to work for their passage in Congress.

Among those meeting with Mr. Johnson were the Rev. Dr. Martin Luther King Jr., president of the Southern Christian Leadership Conference; Roy Wilkins, executive secretary of the National Association for the Advancement of Colored People; A. Philip Randolph, president of the Negro American Labor Council and a member of the executive council of the American Federation of Labor and Congress of Industrial Organizations; Floyd R. McKissick, director of the Congress of Racial Equality; Miss Dorothy Height, president of the National Council of Negro Women; Joseph L. Rauh, general counsel of the Leadership Conference on Civil Rights, and David Brody, director of the Washington office of the Anti-Defamation League.

Representative Emanuel Celler, Democrat of Brooklyn, who is chairman of the House Judiciary Committee, also attended the meeting.

He said that his committee would begin hearings on the President's proposals on Wednesday with Attorney General Katzenbach as the first witness.

Mr. Katzenbach said that he thought the President's proposals would be passed by Congress, but added: "I'm not going to give long odds on it until I know how the Republican leaders are going to go."

The Attorney General said that the Republican leaders had not indicated that they were going to oppose the proposals, nor have they given their commitment to support them.

He indicated that he had kept in close touch with the Senate minority leader, Everett McKinley Dirksen of Illinois, during the drafting of the legislation. Mr. Katzenbach said that the Senator had indicated that he liked some of the proposals, but had questions about others.

Senator Sam J. Ervin Jr., Democrat of North Carolina, quickly attacked the housing provisions of Mr. Johnson's message.

"It's unconstitutional according to all decisions handed down by the Supreme Court during the first 150 years of its existence and it's unenforceable," he said. "It is not aimed solely at the South. Its impact may be felt more strongly in other areas of the country. It should be most interesting to watch the politics or the debate now that others' oxen are being gored."

The bill incorporating the intent of the President's message declares it to be the policy of the United States to prevent "discrimination on account of race, color, religion or national origin in the purchase, rental, lease, financing, use and occupancy of housing throughout the nation."

The bill would make it unlawful for anyone engaged in the sale or lease of a dwelling, including real estate agents or brokers to refuse to sell or rent because of race, color, religion or national origin. Nor could they discriminate in the conditions of sale or rental or represent for discriminatory purposes that any dwelling was not available for inspection, sale or rental when that was not so.

DAMAGES PROVIDED

The prohibitions would be enforced by civil actions in Federal or state courts brought by private individuals or, where a pattern of discrimination appeared to exist, by the Justice Department. Courts would be empowered to issue orders banning discrimination and, on a showing that discrimination had been practiced, award damages of up to $500.

The bill would leave in operation state and local fair housing laws.

The new criminal statute proposed by the President is aimed at what he called "a relatively few racial fanatics" who would deny civil rights by violence.

The Federal laws covering this area were passed during the Reconstruction period after the Civil War, with maximum prison terms of 10 years. The Justice Department has found them inadequate.

The President proposed that any interference in the exercise of fundamental rights by threats or force by any person, acting individually or in a group, privately or officially, be made a Federal crime.

The rights specifically enumerated are voting, education, housing, employment, jury service and travel.

Maximum penalties would be one year in prison and a $1,000 fine in cases where no bodily injury was done, 10 years in prison and a $10,000 fine where there was bodily injury and life imprisonment when death resulted.

Senate Approves Civil Rights Bill by 71-to-20 Vote

BY MARJORIE HUNTER | MARCH 12, 1968

WASHINGTON, MARCH 11 — The Senate passed today a sweeping civil rights bill that would strike down racial barriers in about 80 per cent of the nation's housing.

The vote was 71 to 20, a stunning victory for the tiny band of scrappy liberals that guided the bill through more than seven weeks of stormy debate.

The scene now shifts to the House, which last year passed a relatively noncontroversial civil rights bill to which the Senate has added open housing and antiriot provisions.

The outlook in the House for the amended bill is uncertain.

President Johnson said that every American "can be proud of the Senate's action today" in affirming "our nation's commitment to human rights under law." He urged quick House approval so that "this bill will soon be before me for signing into law."

The House could accept the Senate version without change, send it to conference to work out the differences between its version and the Senate's, or amend the Senate version on the floor and return it to the Senate for further action there.

PROVISIONS OF BILL

As passed by the Senate, the bill would do the following:

- Prohibit discrimination by three stages, in the sale or rental of about 52.6 million of the nation's 65 million housing units.

- Provide penalties of up to 10 years in prison and a $10,000 fine for persons convicted of intimidating or injuring civil rights workers and Negroes in housing, schooling, jury duty, public facilities, voting or registering to vote. This is the sole provision of the House-passed bill.

• Make it a Federal crime to travel from one state to another — or use a radio, television or other interstate facilities — with the intent to incite a riot. The House approved similar provisions last year, but in a separate bill. A riot was defined as a public disturbance, involving three or more persons and endangering either people or property.

• Make it a Federal crime to manufacture, transport in interstate commerce or demonstrate the use of firearms, firebombs or other explosive devices meant for use in a riot or other civil disorder.

• Make it a Federal crime to obstruct firemen or policemen engaged in a riot.

• Extend broad rights to American Indians in their dealings with tribal governments, the courts and local, state and Federal governments. A similar bill passed the Senate last year, but it did not clear the House Interior Committee.

Housing barriers would be lowered by three stages:

• Effective upon passage, would bar discrimination in the sale or rental of Federally owned and multiunit dwellings whose mortgages were insured or underwritten by the Federal Housing Administration and the Veterans Administration.

• Effective Dec. 31, would bar discrimination in multiunit housing, such as apartments, and in real estate developments. Owner-occupied dwellings of four or less units would be excluded.

• Effective Jan. 1, 1970, would bar discrimination in single-family houses sold or rented through brokers. Only if the owner sold the home himself, without aid of a broker, could he discriminate.

The Department of Housing and Urban Development would be authorized to attempt conciliation. If that failed, civil suits could be brought by individuals or the Attorney General.

Startled by the decisiveness of the Senate vote, House leaders of both parties met separately to discuss what course to take.

Speaker John W. McCormack of Massachusetts reported later that the Democratic leadership was still attempting to work out its strategy.

The House Republican leader, Gerald R. Ford of Michigan, said after a meeting with his leadership team that he was undecided whether to support the Senate changes.

Mr. Ford opposed a more limited open housing proposal approved by the House two years ago by a vote of 222 to 190. That bill died in the Senate later that year.

Without substantial support from the 187 House Republicans, Democratic leaders hold out little hope for approval of open housing.

There are 246 House Democrats, but more than 80 of them are Southerners strongly opposed to open housing. Furthermore, some Democrats from Northern cities have expressed misgivings over open housing, primarily because they fear white backlash.

The strong Republican showing in the Senate for open housing could be influential in winning substantial Republican support in the House.

Only four Republicans — two of them Southerners — voted against passage today, while two others paired against the bill. Also voting against were 16 Southern Democrats. There are 64 Democrats and 36 Republicans in the Senate.

The long Senate debate, which had centered largely on open housing, ended on a surprisingly quiet note. Opponents made no further effort to block action.

The few liberals who had guided the bill to passage appeared to be emotionally drained. They made no speeches.

But in a statement issued after passage, Senator Philip A. Hart, Democrat of Michigan, who was floor leader of the bill, said his feelings "might best be described as those of mingled surprise and gratitude."

The issue, he said, was one that the Senate might have avoided. Since "hardly anyone expected anything else."

"There was no groundswell of influential support for fair housing," he said. "Clergymen were not packing the corridors outside the chamber. Civil rights leaders across the nation had not zeroed in on this issue with mighty unanimity."

Senator Hart said that many who voted for the bill "would have been politically more comfortable if the issue had crept away to a quiet death." But he said the Senate responded "to the demands of history" because "it was the right thing to do."

Others who had led the fight for a strong bill were Senators Walter F. Mondale, Democrat of Minnesota; and Jacob K. Javits of New York and Edward W. Brooke of Massachusetts both Republicans.

As originally proposed, the bill would have been limited to Federal protection of civil rights workers and Negroes. Liberals later sought to add provisions that would have barred discrimination in 97 per cent of the dwelling units.

These were scaled down after negotiations between the liberals and Senator Everett McKinley Dirksen of Illinois, the Senate Republican leader, who had opposed open housing but changed his position.

Explaining his shift, Senator Dirksen told the Senate today that only 21 states now had open housing laws. Expressing the fear that it might take 15 to 20 years for the other 29 states to follow suit, Senator Dirksen pounded his fist on his desk and cried: "This free land cannot wait that long."

New U.S. Job Plan for Negroes Set

BY ROY REED | JULY 18, 1969

WASHINGTON, JULY 17 — A new Federal effort to increase Negro employment in the construction trades will go into effect tomorrow in the Philadelphia area, barring a last-minute adverse ruling by the Controller General.

Known as the "Philadelphia Plan," the new approach will be expanded to other cities and other industries if it succeeds in Philadelphia.

Federal contractors bidding on construction jobs will be required to agree to employ given numbers of minority workers — perhaps three to five Negro carpenters, for example — before they can get a contract.

The plan, devised by the Labor Department as part of its equal employment program, has been praised by Whitney M. Young Jr., executive director of the National Urban League, as a possible model for the rest of the nation.

THOSE COVERED BY PLAN

It will apply to iron workers, plumbers, pipefitters, steamfitters, sheet metal workers, electrical workers, roofers, waterproofers and elevator construction workers.

A similar plan last year had to be abandoned because it ran afoul of Federal laws on bidding.

Arthur Fletcher, Assistant Secretary of Labor, who signed the new order, said today the new approach had been approved by lawyers of the Labor and Justice Departments. It still must be approved by the Controller General.

The plan, however, is opposed by several conservative Senators, including Everett McKinley Dirksen of Illinois, the Republican leader, and John L. McClellan, the Arkansas Democrat.

An aide to Senator Dirksen said that the opposing Senators might introduce legislation to block the effort if the Labor Department went ahead with its plan.

NO FIGURE REQUIREMENTS

The Senators contend that requiring a contractor to employ a certain number of minority workers is the same as imposing a quota, and quotas are prohibited by the Civil Rights Act of 1964.

The Labor and Justice Department lawyers argue not only that the plan is consistent with the 1964 law, but also that it does not even draw its power from that law but from Executive order No. 11246 requiring equal employment clauses in all Federal contracts.

The original Philadelphia Plan did not impose figure requirements in the bid advertisements. It relied instead on negotiations with the contractors after bids were submitted. The Controller General ruled against it on the ground that this interposed a new cost factor after bids were compiled.

The new plan was modified somewhat by Secretary of Labor George P. Shultz after the criticism from the Senate. He inserted a clause saying a contractor would not be held to the employment figure in the bid if he could prove he had made a "good faith" effort to hire minority workers and could not do so.

The plan depends heavily on the work of a staff member from the Labor Department's Office of Federal Contract Compliance. He will go to Philadelphia, survey the labor market and decide how many minority workers are available in each category and how many should be hired on each Federal job.

Philadelphia Plan: How White House Engineered Major Victory

BY ROBERT B. SEMPLE JR. | DEC. 26, 1969

WASHINGTON, DEC. 25 — It was near midnight last Monday, and the Senate, in a major reversal of sentiment, had just voted to give the Administration authority to compel labor unions to hire more Negroes.

A weary Senator, Jacob K. Javits, who was walking out of the chamber two minutes after the vote, caught a glimpse of a Presidential aide, Leonard Garment, and tossed a quick remark over his shoulder:

"You see now what we can do up here when the President gives some leadership. We can practically accomplish miracles."

The Senate vote that evening was the climax of a bitter, uphill and largely unreported Administration struggle to salvage the Philadelphia Plan, a Labor Department program designed to encourage more Negro employment in the construction trades.

LIFE AFTER THREE DEATHS

The plan died three times: In a Senate committee Wednesday night, on the Senate floor Thursday and in a joint House-Senate conference committee Saturday. Then, on Monday evening, the House overturned the conference committee action and forced the Senate to reverse its own position a few hours later.

If Senator Javits was cheered by the victory, the Administration was elated.

Accused by his critics of ambiguous leadership, the President had rallied his forces in a moment of legislative crisis and had won a major victory. Suspected in the North of pandering to the South, the Administration may have reopened channels of communications with a Negro community that had all but lost hope in it. Criticized for poor liaison and inefficient communications with its allies in Congress, the White House staff had indicated that it could mobilize diverse resources — including unnatural allies like the Americans for Democratic Action — to bargain successfully for votes.

To some more skeptical folk, the victory was less a tribute to the President's skill than a reflection of the latent forces in Congress that are ready at any time to support meaningful civil rights legislation.

LAST-MINUTE TONIC

Whatever the meaning of the outcome of the week-long struggle, the victory provided a last-minute tonic for the President and his men before they closed their first difficult year with Congress and made arrangements to leave for San Clemente, Calif., to prepare for another.

As reconstructed from a dozen sources inside and outside the Administration, the campaign started in midsummer, when the Administration proposed the Philadelphia plan as a forerunner of similar programs in other cities. The plan would require bidders on federally assisted projects costing more than $500,000 to work toward "specific goals" for improving minority employment in the craft unions, where only 8.4 per cent of 1.3 million union members are black.

A contractor would not have to meet all of these goals if he could prove "good faith" efforts to hire more Negroes during the life of the contract. Attorney General John N. Mitchell said last summer that this did not set racial employment quotas in violation of the Civil Rights Act of 1964.

Later, however, Controller General Elmer Staats ruled that the plan did violate the act. It was this ruling, plus behind-the-scenes lobbying by the craft unions, that enticed Congress into its first negative action.

RIDER APPROVED

Late Wednesday night, Dec. 17, the Senate Appropriations Committee, dominated by Southerners, voted to attach a rider, or extraneous amendment, to a supplemental appropriations bill specifying that no funds could be spent on any program or contract that the Controller General thought to be in violation of Federal law.

The next morning, Secretary of Labor George P. Shultz, one of the architects of the plan, took the news of the setback to a White House meeting that included Donald Rumsfeld, director of the antipoverty program; Robert H. Finch, the Secretary of Health, Education and Welfare; Daniel Patrick Moynihan, the President's counselor, and the President.

The President was said to have told the participants: "I want the action reversed."

There was, however, no clear strategy for doing so.

"A lot of us," recalled one participant, "really didn't know what had hit us. The committee action had come as a complete surprise."

THREE DECISIONS

Yet even in disarray, the Nixon forces, quarterbacked by the President, managed to produce three important decisions Thursday: To concentrate their lobbying efforts in the House (nobody doubted that the Senate would approve the rider that evening); to emphasize the civil rights rather than the constitutional implications of the struggle, and to give the problem White House visibility.

The Senate met that evening and delivered two crushing blows. It accepted the rider by a 73-to-13 vote and rejected, 52 to 35, a Mitchell-written amendment designed to permit the Philadelphia Plan to continue while the constitutional struggle between the Executive and Mr. Staats was being resolved in the courts.

For the White House, there were two bright moments in an otherwise gloomy day.

First, John W. Gardner, head of the Urban Coalition, authorized the use of his and the coalition's prestige in the fight to save the plan. It was the first visible sign that important constituencies outside the White House were prepared to help.

Second, before the evening was out, John Ehrlichman, the President's assistant for domestic affairs, called Mr. Garment, the President's special consultant on civil rights, and told him the civil rights community was missing from the forces striving to revive the plan. Mr. Garment, one of the few members of the White House staff with real ties to the black community, started jotting down a list of people to call.

LOBBYING TASKS SET

Early Friday morning, the White House staff met to parcel out lobbying responsibilities. Bryce N. Harlow, the President's counselor and legislative aide, was to approach his sources in the House; Mr. Rumsfeld, a former Representative, would telephone as many people as he knew; Mr. Garment would do what he could in the civil rights community.

At some point in the meeting, Mr. Ehrlichman suggested drafting a Presidential statement outlining the civil rights issues involved in the rider. The statement, released later that day, declared that "the civil rights policy to which this Administration is committed is one of demonstrable deeds — one of the things that counts most is earning power."

Mr. Harlow's most immediate worry was the Senate-House conference committee meeting scheduled for the next day. He felt that the committee was stacked against the Philadelphia Plan and sensed that it would quickly ratify the Senate's decision.

But he also knew that the House, which had never actually voted as a body on the Philadelphia Plan, would have to meet Monday to accept or reject the conference committee's decision. Accordingly, he sent some of his aides to talk to House members and, in particular, to Speaker John W. McCormack, Democrat of Massachusetts.

LOBBYISTS MEET

As one of Mr. Harlow's messengers entered Mr. McCormack's office, he saw Andrew Biemiller, chief lobbyist for the American Federation of Labor and Congress of Industrial Organizations, emerging from the Speaker's office. Mr. Biemiller put on his coat, smiled at the Nixon envoy and said:

"I'm sorry, I'm afraid we've got this one."

It turned out to be a premature judgment.

The conference committee, as anticipated, approved the supplemental appropriations bill with the damaging rider. Yet the White House kept its sights trained on the House vote scheduled for Monday.

As the conference committee was voting, Mr. Shultz and his assistant secretary, Arthur Fletcher, a Negro, appeared on television.

"Gentlemen," Mr. Fletcher told newsmen assembled in the office of Ronald L. Ziegler, Mr. Nixon's press secretary, "the name of the game is to put some economic flesh and bones on Dr. [Martin Luther] King's dream."

AID IN RIGHTS COMMUNITY

By Saturday afternoon, Mr. Garment had reached key people in the civil rights community. Roy Wilkins, head of the National Association for the Advancement of Colored People, would make known his support of the plan. Whitney M. Young Jr. of the Urban League would issue a statement, and Joseph Rauh Jr., general counsel for the Leadership Conference on Civil Rights and vice chairman for civil rights of the Americans for Democratic Action, agreed to call his friends on Capitol Hill.

Some of those who worked in the President's behalf say now that they were skeptical of his motives. They did not doubt, they say, his commitment to minority employment, but they have privately suggested that he might have sensed political profit in pitting the civil rights movement against its natural allies in the labor movement.

The White House denies this, asserting that the President gave no thought to the politics involved and was moved largely by a genuine fear that repeal of the Philadelphia Plan would mean the destruction of the strategy for increased minority employment.

Whatever his motives, the President clearly wanted the plan preserved. On Sunday, after a White House church service, he called the Wednesday action by the Senate committee "dirty pool," and on Monday morning he presided over what participants described as one of the most extraordinary leadership meetings of this or any other Administration.

NO ORDINARY AFFAIR

Weeks before, the President had invited the wives of Congressional leaders to accompany their husbands to a leadership breakfast. It was to have been a relaxed and ordinary affair.

It was neither. As the wives filed in they saw Mr. Mitchell, Mr. Shultz and Mr. Fletcher at a table in the State Dining Room.

The President opened with a few remarks, then Mr. Fletcher gave an off-the-cuff talk that participants later described as "brilliant."

He poured out statistics on minority employment in the craft unions, pointing out that of the 1.3 million workers employed in the $24-billion space program, fewer than 4 per cent were black. He ended by saying that if "this is stopped here, it will be stopped all across the country."

Later, Senator Gorden Allott, Republican of Colorado, addressed himself to the Attorney General.

He said that he had been an early and ardent advocate of civil rights but that he now found himself "sick at heart" because, in his mind, the real issue was constitutional: Congress, heeding its Controller General, had pronounced the Philadelphia Plan in defiance of the Civil Rights Act, and he did not think he could support it.

Mr. Mitchell argued that the plan required no strict "quotas," and the President said that he appreciated Mr. Allott's views but that the plan was central to his whole effort to get people working.

After the meeting, events moved very swiftly.

The House and Senate Republican leaders, Gerald R. Ford of Michigan and Hugh Scott of Pennsylvania, delivered a pep talk to newsmen.

White House aides and their recruited allies — most notably, Mr. Rauh — deployed to the waiting rooms off the House chamber. The President issued another statement.

WHITE HOUSE VICTORY

In early evening, the House voted 208 to 156 to reject the controversial rider; the Senate followed suit four hours later by a margin of 39 to 29.

The President stayed in his office, according to aides, until midnight, quietly awaiting each fresh piece of news.

Meanwhile, Mr. Rauh and Mr. Garment watched the voting from the gallery. When a prominent liberal would vote for the Philadelphia Plan, Mr. Garment would nod appreciatively toward Mr. Rauh. And when a prominent conservative would vote the same way — Mr. Rauh recalls, in particular, the ballot of Wallace Bennett of Utah — he would nod in Mr. Garment's direction.

"The point," Mr. Rauh now says, "is that this Administration can reach the people we can't — the Republican middle. This means that any time the Administration is for civil rights it can win — even against labor. That is the hopeful thing to emerge from this episode."

After Nine Years — A Homecoming for the First Black Girl at the University of Georgia

BY CHARLAYNE HUNTER | JAN. 25, 1970

ATHENS, GA. — Several days after Hamilton (Hamp) Holmes and I entered the University of Georgia in 1961 under court order as its first two black students, I sat in a world history class, fighting desperately to stay awake and avoid confirming the stereotype that all blacks are lazy. The drowsiness was the result of my first few days on campus when white students, protesting our admission, rioted outside my dormitory.

Shortly after a brick and bottle had shattered the window in my room, sending chunks of broken glass within a foot of where I was standing, Hamilton, who lived off campus, and I were suspended for our "own safety." Our lawyers got the judge who had ordered us in to order us readmitted, but the girls who lived above me — I was the sole resident on the first floor — continued for a long time to pound the floor, night after night, late into the night, and I suffered the physical and mental exhaustion of those first few days throughout the winter quarter. Somehow, it was always in this mid morning history class that I would find myself embarrassed as my head drooped and my eyes closed.

Almost nine years later, during my first visit to the campus since graduation, I entered that same classroom — this time wide awake, and found not a course in world history, but one in African history, part of a new black-studies program; and not one exhausted black girl, but five outspoken black men and women among the students and a young black man, with a heavy Afro haircut and wearing a turtleneck sweater, teaching the course. By the end of the hour, as the white students sat quietly taking notes, the black instructor was acting as referee for two of the black students who were engaged in a vehement clash of opinion on the subject of pan-Africanism.

BETTMANN/GETTY IMAGES

Charlayne Hunter and Hamilton Holmes, right, en route to the University of Georgia registrar's office to become the first Negroes ever to enroll at the state-supported institution. They arrived shortly after the registrar opened Jan. 9, 1961, armed with court orders to ensure their admission.

"YOU WON'T BELIEVE your eyes when you see the changes," a Georgia English professor had told me when I called her from New York to say that I was coming to Athens. Then the professor, who, when I was a student, had lived in an apartment directly across the street, which she offered as a refuge whenever I needed it, went on to issue a warning: "Come on down; just remember the stir you caused last time."

We both laughed. Nonetheless, as I stepped off the bus at the dingy little station a block from the campus, I felt a slight wave of anxiety sweep over me. But before I could dwell on that, I heard someone call my name. Looking around, I saw a familiar face, although I couldn't place it.

"I thought it was you," the man said, extending his hand. "I'm Pete Sasser from the journalism school." Pete had been a student there when I entered, and although I was a journalism major, I had little contact with the students when I was there, and have had almost none since I graduated. Pete said he was on the faculty now, and invited me over to see the new journalism school. I told him that I had heard that the dean had retired, but that I hadn't known that the old building had been retired, too. We settled on 3 o'clock, which would leave me time to have lunch with some professor friends and to get from them some suggestions about whom I should see this time around. I had my own ideas about whom I did not want to see.

Again, at lunch, I was told how impressed I would be with the changes. One of the group, my former classics professor, Ed Best, had just returned from the University of Alabama, where he had served as a judge in the Miss Homecoming contest. Among the contestants, he told me, were a Japanese girl and a black girl with an Afro, and they both finished in the top three, although Alabama was not ready for either one to reign as queen.

"You won't find anything like that here," Dr. Best said, "but I do think you'll find some things have changed."

After lunch, armed with a list of other names and places, I left the Holiday Inn and headed across the street to the first building I had ever set foot in at the university to have a talk with the new acting dean of student affairs, a young white Alabamian named O. Suthern Sims.

On my way over, I caught a glimpse of the Kappa Alpha house. It had been one of several trouble spots which I generally tried to avoid. The fraternity brothers of K.A. could always be counted on to yell at least one mouthful of obscenities if Hamp or I was passing by their house. Most of the time, we pretended to ignore them.

But every now and then, they would rile the normally calm, easy-going Hamp, and he would say, "Just look at the way they treat that flag they're supposed to love so much," referring to the Confederate flag. "They couldn't be serious the way they leave it out in all kinds of wind and rain." Even though it was a symbol of disgust to both of us, I think Hamp would have respected them a little more if they had shown some respect for what they were supposed to cherish. Now, there it was, tattered and rotting, but still flying.

Across the street and inside the academic building where Hamp and I had registered for our first classes, Dean Sims was a welcome change from the tight-jawed, closed-minded segregationists who preceded him. Tall and slender and articulate, he greeted me warmly and said he hoped I had so far found the university to be a lot different from what it had been when I first came. I smiled noncommittally because I had not yet talked with any of the black students on campus, and urged him, instead, to tell me if he thought it had.

"We've now moved almost 180 degrees in regard to the psychology of *in loco parentis*," he said, and proceeded to outline the liberalization that had taken place in rules for students, particularly women, which had prohibited them from living off campus, staying out past 11 P.M. and wearing slacks. I found all this interesting, since along with the loosening up had come an end to the offices of dean of men and dean of women — in my years as a student there, the very personification of *in loco parentis*, particularly for Hamp and me, their unwanted children.

When after two and a half years in one isolated room in a freshman dormitory, I had asked for a transfer to an upper-class dorm, it was the dean of women's office that said it couldn't be done — not because of segregation, but out of "consideration." Dean Edith Stallings told Calvin Trillin, a friend who helped me maintain my sanity while covering my entrance and who came back later to write a book about it: "We don't like to put any student in a position where she's not wanted. It's not race."

Her counterpart, Dean William E. Tate, took much of the credit for "protecting" Hamp and me during our stay there. I never had much to say to him, nor he to me, but he always seemed quite fond of Hamp. I was told that he often spoke of "Holmes," telling of Hamp's initiation into Phi Beta Kappa — an invitation which Tate himself extended by letter — as if he were his own.

By the end of this year, both will have been retired. "Tate has accepted this thing beautifully," Sims said. "He has a truly wonderful capacity to adapt."

AND WHAT ABOUT the capacity of the university to adapt to the presence of black students beyond the number of two, and without pressure from the courts?

Suthern Sims paused briefly, then said: "I think you can think of the integration of blacks into the university in two ways — legally and attitudenally. There is no question in terms of all the proper compliances. I do not believe you can find any forms of racial segregation that you can take any legal action against. I've looked for it, especially in student affairs. It's just not there."

He went on to outline the areas governed by Federal compliance regulations: "We will not list an apartment or job unless a compliance form is signed. We don't have any black rooms like they once had. To the best of my knowledge that stopped in '67." (My mind flashed back to my senior year when I had wanted Donald Hollowell, our lawyer, to go back to court for an order to desegregate the dorms. At that time, he had so many civil-rights cases pending, including some of Dr. Martin Luther King's, that he just didn't have the time and probably thought it wasn't worth it. I think the black students who eventually did have to push it five years later would have disagreed.)

In addition, Sims pointed out, of a total of 200 resident advisers — young women who live in the dorms, are paid $650 a year and offer non-professional guidance to their fellow students — five are black. "We hired every one that applied," Sims said, not altogether unconscious of the two ways in which the remark could be taken.

"AS TO ATTITUDE," Sims said slowing down a little, "I can't measure it." Then he brought up the subject of the Black Student Union. In nine years, the university population has increased from about 7,200 students to about 18,000, with the number of blacks growing from two to "approximately 125" (no one admits to knowing for sure just how many black students there are). About 75 blacks are undergraduates, and of the total — including graduate students — about 30 belong to the B.S.U. For two consecutive years, the group has presented demands to the university administration.

"I think what they're really talking about is attitude, and this is a tough one," Sims said. "This might sound awfully inept, but I think it's improving. This current generation is the finest generation of college students that this country has ever seen. They've been more right about more issues than any before them. And here is where I think you'll find the meshing of legality and attitude."

He continued: "Our blacks come in and they're experiencing disgust and hostility, and it becomes really a paradox — 'You do something about it now,' they say. But we can't just unilaterally rule against attitude. That's a fascist state." Back to 1961, in my memory: the white students who vowed not to accept desegregation, despite the fact that it was "being shoved down our throats." "You can't legislate morality," they were fond of saying.

Sims's personal assessment of the B.S.U. was, in general, favorable. He was but one of several administrators who conceded that without its pressure, some of the changes that were taking place within the university "probably wouldn't have happened so fast."

"I think I understand what they want," Sims said finally. "They want role models, not tokens." Then he pointed out what he considered gains in that area — blacks hold clerical positions throughout the university; there is even one in administration; there are black "public-safety officers." There are the five resident advisers.

But there were some ideas proposed by the B.S.U. that Dean Sims simply could not reconcile with his own personal code. He said they had asked for a separate dormitory and had refused to bring the organization officially on campus because they did not want to sign the compliance. "They told me frankly that, if they signed the compliance, they'd have to let whites in, and they don't want that.

"I make no bones about it. I'm an integrationist, not a separatist, because if you buy the separatist bag in the South, you positively re-enforce the white supremists. And to buy that would be to step back 75 years."

NEXT DAY, I stopped by the office of the dean of arts and sciences. He was not in, so I talked briefly with his assistant, Dr. Charles Wynes. Dr. Wynes had been in the history department when I was a student; since then, he has written a book, "The Negro in America Since 1865."

Dr. Wynes said that the university has really moved fast over the past few years. As evidence of the growth, he cited an appropriation by the State Legislature to increase the faculty by more than 500, citing it as "a breakthrough for educational excellence."

As I stood to leave, it occurred to me to ask Dr. Wynes how many of the 500 new faculty members were blacks. He said there was one, Dr. Richard Graham, a musical therapist.

My next stop was at the building where Dean Sims had told me I could find Ben Colebert, a young black who is also a kind of first. Although he is a graduate student in the art department, he is the first black admissions counselor, and it is his job to travel throughout the state to recruit black students.

A handsome medium brown, with a quiet Afro, Colebert, who is 27, moved with ease in what I was surprised to find was the office of M. O. Phelps. At the time Hamp and I were trying to get in, Phelps was freshman admissions counselor. I didn't have any problems with him in person, but he was one of a panel of three administrators who decided, on the basis of their interview with Hamp, that he was "not a suitable candidate" for admission.

In addition to the fact that he did not say "Sir," they said that he slumped in his chair, gave short answers to their questions, mumbled when he spoke and left them with "some doubt about his truthfulness." Hamp had a slight speech impediment, which often caused him to stutter or hesitate before he spoke.

Colebert said Phelps "admitted he had some prejudices," but that among the many dinner invitations he and his wife had received was one from Phelps.

"They really smoked me over," Ben said when I asked how he got the job. "I think they wanted to see how militant I was, but right away I knew I was the kind of nigger they wanted. In 1959, I did sit-ins, when I was an undergraduate at Savannah State. But that was a decade ago, and I don't have my master's yet, so I made myself very attractive to them."

Ben and I are the same age, and when he was sitting in at lunch counters in Savannah, I had just applied to the university. By the time I was admitted, it was 1961, and Ben, like me, would have been a sophomore. But he told me during my visit that he was encountering among black high-school students in the state the same problem he had had — as late as the year we graduated: "I simply didn't know the school existed, and neither do they."

ONCE THEY KNOW, there is the problem of money. Even though the university is state-supported, expenses for an on-campus student can be $2,000 a year or more. "It *does* cost a lot of money," Ben said, "but there's a lot in this institution that needs to be channeled into the black community. The black community pays taxes, and supports this school." He added that 80 per cent of the black students at the university receive either work-study or graduate assistanceships or Federal aid. "If you have the guts to come here in the first place, then you got it made," he said.

(That wasn't necessarily so in my case, despite the rumor that the N.A.A.C.P. was paying me $50 a day. If I had been in it for the money that would hardly have been enough, but the rumor was totally groundless. The N.A.A.C.P. Legal Defense and Educational Fund donated its talents to fight our legal battles — but its support ended there, as it should have. Carl Holman, my closest friend, now a vice president of the National Urban Coalition, who was then a professor at Clark

College and the editor of The Atlanta Inquirer, managed each quarter through friends to wangle some money from such groups as the Elks of Memphis, who paid the $83 a quarter or thereabouts for my room in the dormitory. And sometimes I made money speaking, although most of those engagements were for church groups that paid with "Praise the Lord" and "God bless you."

(It never occurred to me to apply for a job on campus, although I had worked at Wayne State University before I transferred. And I'm not sure that with all the other pressures at that time I would have been able to handle a job, too. Nor did I think of applying for any kind of loan or aid. Having had to force my way in, I guess I couldn't imagine their doing anything to help me stay.)

ADMISSION REQUIREMENTS have stood in the way of black applicants, according to Ben Colebert. For starters, a combined score of 900 on the nationwide Scholastic Aptitude Test (S.A.T.) is required, in addition to a B-plus average. "The black school system just hasn't been geared toward passing these tests," he explained. "In a dual school system, black kids don't usually even come out with a foreign language. These tests are geared for kids who go to white, middle-class high schools. If a black kid does succeed in making 900 on the S.A.T., you know he could have made 1,500 with the proper background."

Most white students are, in addition, more test-conscious than blacks, having prepared for at least a couple of years for the S.A.T. by taking old tests and using books with prepared tests in them. My high school was one of the few black schools that did that when I was preparing for college. We had sessions for several weeks, on Saturday mornings, but my scores were still horrible. Fortunately, I never made below a B in any of my courses, and graduated third in my class. This, according to Colebert, would make a difference today, even with a low score.

At present, the mean score for the entire university for boys is 1,050, and for girls, about 1,060. "Less than half of 1 per cent" of the black students, according to Colebert, have even a 900 score. Their presence is the result of an admissions committee's recommendations. "The university does make some concessions," Colebert said.

I asked him about the football players — whites, many of whom could barely speak English. Surely they didn't have 900 S.A.T. scores. Colebert laughed. "We don't get into that," he said.

Because of inferior preparation, many black students have difficulties with their courses, particularly English — a bane to most Southern freshmen, regardless of color. Many of them flunked out. The B.S.U. demanded that they be readmitted, and that some special counseling program be set up. President Fred C. Davison responded in this way: "The admission and re-admission policies of the university are conducted without regard to race. The proposal to readmit all black students who have flunked out of the university is not only educationally unsound but it, too, could be challenged on the grounds of racial discrimination. Moreover, such a policy would result in a serious impairment of academic standards the university."

Ben does not think that the liberal grants to black students will continue for long — "particularly if they get a lot of black students." However, he plans to continue recruiting. "It *is* ironic," he said as I was leaving, "that now that the University of Georgia is concerned with admitting black students, comes the insurgence of pride in black institutions and black environments."

"How do you deal with that?" I asked.

"The only thing I tell them is that you get more awareness of being black here than in a black institution where it's taken for granted." It was a theme that I later heard expressed again and again by black students here.

GRADUALLY, I MADE my way to the history department, which houses the black studies program. I knew that there I would get not only some idea about the program, but also would probably run into some of the black students. Although 125 certainly increases the odds of coming across a black student, they still manage to get lost on the sprawling campus among 18,000 whites.

While waiting for Dr. David Foley, the young white professor in charge of the program, I looked at the paper. That morning, The Athens Daily News carried the headline: "Black Studies Panel Hears Local Professor," with a story out of Atlanta, which began: "While most speakers agreed Monday that more emphasis on black studies is needed in the state's public schools, a University of Georgia department head said this might result in building 'feelings of superiority among blacks.' " The man, who was quoted later in the story as saying that Negro history taught distinctly "could backfire badly," is chairman of the social studies department.

Dr. Foley, who taught for three years at the University of Sierra Leone, turned out to be pleasant, enthusiastic and intensely pleased with himself. "In most universities," he said, "whites ignore the existence of black culture. They're not anti — they just spend their time saying, 'What a wonderful fellow I am.' This is more degrading than anything. I don't know whether a black would like somebody to just come up and whack 'im one or ignore him."

Foley feels that students "cannot understand the demands or aspirations of Afro-Americans without an understanding of the black man as the inheritor of African culture." As for his own preparation, he said, "I'd like to think my two years in Africa helped me to rap here."

Downstairs, in an African history classroom, Anderson Williams, a young black graduate assistant who had just passed his Ph.D. orals, was lecturing on the "strong indigenous civilization in Africa that began a thousand years before the Europeans came to the continent."

After the class ended, I introduced myself to the black students sitting in front of me, and invited them to have lunch with me. Anderson Williams joined us, and we drove to a steak house in town — one of many that did not serve black people when I graduated.

On the way out, Benny Roberson, a junior from Athens, majoring in anthropology, started to chuckle. "Charlayne Hunter. You know how I remember you so well? The day you entered Georgia and all that stuff was going on with you, I started getting ready to go to town, and my mamma said, 'Boy, you are not going *nowhere* near that town *today*.' And I sat back down."

"When I first came here," said Joe Sales, a handsome senior from Columbus, Ga., who reminded me of Hamp, "I knew every black student on the yard, but not now."

Russell Williams, a graduate student who had been at the university off and on, having started his freshman year when I was a senior, concurred, and added, "There are even some black students nobody knows."

They explained that, although they and about 30 other black students belonged to the B.S.U., the majority did not. And while, they said, many of those who were not members sympathized, there were others who would not have anything to do with them.

Then Joe said: "You see, there's a basic division between those students who come from predominantly black schools and people who went to a white high school. The ones who went to a white high school are more willing to relate."

"Still," Russell interjected, "even those who participate are, at best, being tolerated. Those are the ones who catch it from both ends."

It was clear that my luncheon companions had no plans to get involved in university life or activities. I asked why. They all started to speak at once. Joe, who emerged strongest, said, "We tried it, but after all this time, we still feel like aliens in a strange land."

THEY EXPLAINED THAT the B.S.U. was formed in 1967 because of that. "At first," Joe continued, "it just provided a social outlet — black-oriented functions. We would all meet at Bob Benham's house and party. It got to be known as 'The Black House.' "

Benham, now in his last year of law school, had been president of the B.S.U. when it presented a list of 22 demands to the university — the first step the B.S.U. took after its members realized that "partying all the time wasn't going to lead to any change in our lives within the university."

"The first year, we were concerned with getting a fair break," Joe explained. "We asked for things like an end to discrimination in housing — black people always ended up in the same rooms — and an end to discrimination in employment — as usual, they try to token you to death. We asked for a wider range of things because the whole idea was not just to represent the militants, but to represent a wide range of political opinion. Like, I'm not interested in fraternities, but the brother here is."

In that connection they asked for a ban on racist fraternities — specifically K.A. "There are still incidents in front of that house," they told me. "Black women are constantly subjected to all kinds of verbal abuse and getting things thrown at them."

DURING THE NEXT YEAR, an expanded set of demands was presented to the university — some in the same vein as the previous year, but some more militant. Some of their optimism had waned. A young freshman from Atlanta, James Hurley, had gone out for football. He made the freshman team, the Bullpups, but as the year wore on and he began looking with anticipation toward playing with the Bulldogs, a sympathetic coach called him aside one day and told him that Georgia would probably dress him, but that if he was really serious about playing football, he'd better look elsewhere. (Subsequently, Vanderbilt offered him a scholarship — and a chance to play — and he took it.)

Among the new demands that year was one for the establishment of a black dormitory. "If asking for an end to discrimination in housing one year, and a black dormitory the next sounds contradictory, it's not," Joe said. Then, talking all at once, they said that the demand was the logical next step to take with a university that says one thing, but does another.

Earlier, Ben Colebert had said it bothered him that some black students would want to request such a thing, but added, "The University should spend less of its energies condemning it, and more trying to find out why they want it." One indication of why might be revealed in the letter President Davison wrote to Benham in response to the demands. The letter, dated March 8, 1969, stated, in part:

"As for the recruitment of athletes, Athletic Director Evans has advised all coaches by memorandum that the university would recruit regardless of race, creed, or color. A Negro student has been designated to receive a tuition and books scholarship in the spring quarter if he is academically eligible to compete. To date, six Negro athletes have been offered full scholarships (three in football, two in track and one in basketball) or would have been had they been academically eligible. ..." This sounded vaguely reminiscent of the series of technicalities on which Hamilton and I were denied admission to the university for a year and a half.

On K.A., President Davison wrote: "Kappa Alpha ... is a duly constituted and recognized social fraternity and is in compliance with the provision of the department of student activities. The university cannot arbitrarily abolish such an organization."

IT SEEMED ALMOST as if the incidence of racism had risen in direct proportion to the number of blacks on campus. Joe put it this way: "To me racism is when you take English 101 and have to read 'Heart of Darkness,' and I point out that it's racist, just like 'Othello,' and the teacher takes points off my essay for it. In short, when you're looking at things from a black perspective, they can't understand it."

Several students at different times told me of a psychology professor who, upon seeing two black girls in his class, launched into a discussion of the high incidence of crime, illegitimacy, syphilis and gonorrhea among black people, and ended by saying that he knew of at least two people who were going to flunk the course. The girls withdrew from the class.

In some instances, escape was not so easy. One sociology major told me of a course required for a master's in his field. It was called "Community Reconnaissance." He was told he could not take the course that time around because it involved a field trip to Oglethorpe County, where the class was to survey community leaders on what they felt was wrong with their communities.

The student, Leonard Lester, called Pie by the other blacks, said that he suspected there weren't any black leaders in the area, but he demanded that he be allowed to take the course. When an alternative — not involving the community reconnaissance — was offered, Pie said: "The professor told me, 'I understand your problem, but sometimes you have to go in the back door.' "

Pie went on: "I blew my stack. Then I went to the head of the department and they finally found some Negroes for me in the county. One was a black school principal, who wouldn't consent to the interview until I shaved my beard off." Pie subsequently dropped out of the university. He said he "just couldn't take it any more."

"The thing about segs," Bob Benham said to me later, "is that they're a lot more sophisticated than they used to be when you were a student. Last year, for instance, I belonged to the Demosthenian Society, and I was elected to the office of custodian. It was my duty to procure things for the organization, open up, and so on. One of the members was Albert Saye, a political-science professor and one of the most notorious segs around. He responded by proposing that the custodian be paid a salary of $20 a quarter."

Bob says he's given up "trying to get along with honkies." Last summer, he, along with several of his classmates, served as an intern in the office of Gov. Lester Maddox. He says he enjoyed it, but he doesn't think he could do it again.

"Time was, when a guy slipped and said 'colored' you'd consider it an accident and let him slide." Benham said. "You excused it even when you showed up for class in a shirt and tie and they responded by saying, 'Hi ya doin', preacher?' Or you'd try to study with them, and the first thing they're talking about was sex and how they'd like a black woman. Then you realize that their attitude toward blacks is still that the majority of them are low-life, slimy dogs, and I'm the exception. Their Booker T."

ALTHOUGH THE BLACK STUDENTS say that what is called a black-studies program this year is what the school already had, plus two new courses, and that it doesn't tell blacks anything they don't already know, they are at least partially responsible for that much of a beginning.

Also, they are responsible for the removal of the segregated bathroom signs. Penny Mickelbury, a striking dark-skinned girl from Atlanta with a Kathleen Cleaver-style Afro, said that she and "a group of the brothers and sisters" went into a university cafeteria "determined that those signs were going to come down." They walked to the head of the food lines, she said, and simply refused to move.

I marveled at the story, even up to this point, since this was a cafeteria frequented by many of the Bulldogs. In my day, Bulldogs were known for their pugnacious character.

At any rate, a few of these types, according to Penny, took exception, and although there's some question as to who actually landed the first blow, it wasn't long before the cafeteria was in an uproar. Most of the whites and a few of the blacks left. Penny and a "few of the brothers," including Pie, remained to do battle.

"I climbed up on top of a table and started throwing forks and knives and trays," she recalled. "Anything I could get my hands on. That's one of the reasons they leave us alone. They think we're crazy. Imagine. Thirty black kids got 18,000 honkies scared to death."

BECAUSE AT LEAST a few of the black students make no secret of their readiness to retaliate, "much of the harassment," they say, "has all but disappeared." And despite the fact that the average black student does not participate in the B.S.U., many have benefitted from their protests. Bendelle Love, a young resident adviser in an all-white dorm, is there as a result of B.S.U. demands. She says she works nearly 40 hours a week advising others on their problems and that, because of the time consumed between that and her studies, she just doesn't have time for meetings. Of her own situation, she said, "There's no static."

Others, I think, feel there are some benefits. Pie and Floyd Williams, a graduate student in art, debated the point one evening. Pie said that all he wants to be is a soldier in the revolution. But Floyd argued that the revolution needs professionals — doctors, lawyers, technicians, even sociologists. The struggle, he said, benefits from those who know well their opposition.

But even the most militant of the black students say that things have improved "a little bit." Some say that the number of whites they can talk to is increasing.

I WAS, OF COURSE, particularly curious about how the white students felt about the blacks. In my own time, I had felt that most of them were too preoccupied with fraternity and sorority parties really to concern themselves about us. And from what I was able to glean from various sources, this is still pretty much the case now.

Rebecca Leet, a junior from Atlanta and news editor of The Red and Black, said that she had talked to many white students who had come from integrated high schools, so that they did not consider Georgia's desegregation unusual. (High-school desegregation began the year after my entrance at the university.) "I just sort of don't feel anything toward them," one freshman from a small Georgia town told her, adding: "But I don't feel anything against them." She said she saw "discrimination emanating, to some extent, from the way people talk about them and stuff."

A prelaw senior said that he had been disappointed last year when he tried to "get a human-relations seminar started." He said it was "a shock to him" that black students wouldn't accept him as being sincerely interested. "What do you do when you're sitting there and you are sincere and he doesn't believe you? Where do you go?" he asked.

(I recalled the all too numerous occasions when I was expected to provide easy answers to such questions as "What can we do?" so that they could go out and say, "Negroes say they want. ...")

But charges made by the B.S.U. are confirmed unintentionally in other circumstances by white students who are neither pro nor con.

"I wouldn't be comfortable if I were black on this campus," one white student said. "There's an awful lot of discrimination. It's just the way people have been raised to feel about blacks," he said.

AT THE END of my visit, of all the people I talked with, Joe Sales, the student who reminded me of Hamp, and Andy Williams, the graduate instructor in the African history class, are on my mind. Both bright and articulate, and by no means crazy — by my standards, at least — they came to the university under no other pressure than the knowledge of their communities that one of theirs had made it to a white school.

Now, with most of that behind them, they are disillusioned. "You'd have a lot more militant black people if they attended schools like this," Joe said. He also said: "A lot of things have happened that made me develop negative attitudes about whites that will be with me the rest of my life.

"Nothing here balances out the things I lost — like the inability to keep up with the tempo of the black community. Like I go home now, and I don't feel the same sense of belonging."

Andy feels that way, too, but desperately wants to "return to a black environment." If offered a job at the university, he says, he wouldn't take it. "I just couldn't function, because I think of the question Malcolm X raised and answered: 'You know what they call a black Ph.D.?'

" 'Nigger.' "

It has been more than six years since I left the University of Georgia and the South, and I am still weighing the things I lost against the things I gained. At one point, I even spent six months in graduate school because I felt I needed to fill in the gaps from the education I received from Georgia. Yet, before the six months were over, I realized that the education I received outside the classroom more than made up for what was lost inside. And, maybe, Joe and Andy will experience this, too.

They were not "firsts" in the sense that Hamp and I were *firsts*. So they are not getting the positive attention that we received from throughout the world. I would be less than honest if I did not admit that many ways were paved for me, at least, because I was a first. (Hamp now has his medical degree and is serving as an Army doctor in Germany.)

But they did come to the university out of the same backgrounds as Hamp and I, children of the black *bourgeoisie*, (mentally) or in fact, protected by the same system that discriminated against us. Joe and Andy are appalled at the treatment they are receiving at the University of Georgia because for the first time in their lives, they are feeling it personally. Discrimination through separate and unequal schooling is not something you feel personally.

I remember resenting to the point of being rude that almost my only visitors in my dormitory were the girls whom no man would look at twice, the wallflowers who came because they had no Saturday dates, the overweight, the bookworms or the religious nuts. Not that there weren't exceptions — and some wonderful ones. But the former were the rule. And often, listening to records at night and dancing with the closet door, I would ignore their knocks because I found the whole charade disgusting.

And yet, I stayed, partly because I knew the world was watching. I think that, at that time, such a commitment was necessary. But the need is greater now, precisely because the world isn't watching. The move of black students to black colleges is fine for those who can afford it. But Benny Roberson lives here in Athens, where there is no black college, and he can't afford to go out of town. Things for blacks may improve now, not because the world is watching, but because there are more Benny Robersons.

The University of Georgia may not have prepared its black students for life in the orthodox way we have come to expect universities to do. But if they leave still unsatisfied with the treatment they received as blacks in a microcosmic white society, then I think the university will have succeeded far better than they may be able to realize now.

CHARLAYNE HUNTER is a reporter for The New York Times.

CHAPTER 3

'Reverse Discrimination' Threatens Progress

The civil rights movement afforded African-Americans new rights and demonstrated the value of affirmative action. However, unique cases and unconventional applications of the policy were received with mixed feelings. It wasn't long before the policy of unification created division among the American people. While many still valued what affirmative action stood for during the 1960s, others viewed it as "reverse discrimination." At the same time, the inconsistent support of presidential administrations and the justice system caused the effectiveness of affirmative action to wane.

Gains Are Made in Federal Drive for Negro Hiring

BY JOHN HERBERS | JAN. 25, 1970

WASHINGTON, JAN. 24 — After several years of slow progress in the Government's efforts to open good-paying jobs for minorities through law and executive action, there are signs of possible breakthroughs in several areas.

Federal officials and others in the field of employment practices cite the following developments:

• The Philadelphia Plan, the Nixon Administration's device for placing more blacks in federally aided construction projects, is being implemented with some success in its test city and has spurred negotiations for "home town solutions" in cities across the country.

• The Administration is moving cautiously to extend some of the features of the Philadelphia Plan, including goals for minority jobs, to virtually all work done under Federal contract.

• As a result of hundreds of lawsuits filed on behalf of minority plaintiffs, a body of law has been built around Title VII of the Civil Rights Act of 1964 that is expected to give new impetus to the national movement by blacks for more job opportunities. Title VII deals with discrimination in private employment practices.

SURVEY COMPLETED

In a related matter, the Equal Employment Opportunity Commission has completed the first comprehensive national survey of minority members in referral unions — those that have hiring halls or that supply quotas of workers for the employer — and has found the nonwhite percentages in the better-paying jobs even lower than had been expected.

The survey, based on reports from about 3,700 local unions, was for 1967, but the commission said there had been little change in the union picture since then. The building trades reported Negro membership as 8.4 per cent, but the vast majority of these members were in the lower-paying categories, such as laborer. In the mechanical trades, only 0.8 per cent of the membership was Negro.

A city-by-city breakdown, which the commission will release through its regional offices next month, shows that in some cities where the Negro populations have been burgeoning in recent years, blacks are barely, if at all, represented in the mechanical trades, such as plumber, sheet metal worker and lather.

The Negro percentages in the mechanical trades ranged from 8.2 per cent in New York to zero in such cities as Houston, Birmingham and Kansas City. Atlanta had 0.1 per cent; Chicago and Cleveland, 0.4, and New Orleans, 0.3.

In referral unions other than the building trades, 12 per cent of the membership was reported to be Negro, but the commission said that in these unions as well as the building trades, the high-paying categories had few Negro members. Building, hotel and restaurant employees and teamsters made up the bulk of the Negro membership.

'PERVASIVE PATTERN'

"As our employer surveys also have shown," said the commission chairman, William H. Brown 3d, "the one pervasive pattern in all of American industry is the inverse relationship between pay and skill levels and minority group employment."

It is against this pattern that the Labor Department, other agencies and civil rights organizations have been moving.

The Philadelphia Plan was put into effect Sept. 23 under a long-standing Executive Order forbidding discrimination in Federal contract work. It was implemented despite the objections of Controller General Elmer B. Staats and some members of Congress, who said it required racial quotas in violation of Title VII of the 1964 act.

Under the plan, contractors bidding on Federal projects are required to agree in advance to make a good-faith effort to employ what the Labor Department considers to be a reasonable number of minority workers in the six skilled crafts.

FEW BLACK STEAMFITTERS

For example, although the population of Philadelphia is about 40 per cent black, Negroes make up less than 0.7 per cent of the membership of the steamfitters unions there.

The Labor Department, finding that many blacks are available and qualified, said that during the next four years the minority percentages of steam fitters on Federal projects should be increased to 20 per cent or more.

The department said today that seven contracts containing the minority goals and totaling $34-million had been let in the Philadelphia area and that others were being processed. Some 80 contractors, however, have contested the plan, and a hearing on their lawsuit is to open in Federal District Court Monday. The Labor Department has welcomed the suit as an opportunity to prove the legality of the plan.

When the plan was put into effect, Secretary of Labor George P. Shultz indicated that it would be expanded to some other cities as the manpower of the department permitted, but he added that "there is no solution like a home town solution."

At that time, pressures from blacks and the Government were mounting in Chicago, where all the building trades had only 3.5 per cent Negro membership.

After heated negotiations, an agreement was reached early this month among the black civic organizations, the unions, the contractors and Mayor Richard J. Daley to provide 4,000 new jobs a year for five years in private and public construction.

SHULTZ PRAISES PACT

Mr. Shultz praised the Chicago agreement, even though it did not contain the guarantees the Labor Department thought were needed to be sure a fair proportion of the jobs would be in the better-paying mechanical trades.

Meantime, Newark and Boston have become the focal points for negotiations and Government pressures. It is considered likely that the Philadelphia Plan will be instituted in those cities if no "home town solution" is reached.

John L. Wilks, director of the Office of Federal Contract Compliance, said the Government policy and pressures by blacks had spurred negotiations in Pittsburgh; St. Louis; Oakland and San Jose, Calif.; Detroit; Atlanta, and other cities. In Seattle, the contractors and minorities have been negotiating, and the Justice Department has filed suits against some of the unions.

While this was going on, Senator Sam J. Ervin, Democrat of North Carolina, a foe of the Philadelphia Plan, charged that the Labor Department was secretly enforcing a new order extending the "quota system" to all Federal contractors. Labor Department spokesmen said that the order, dated last Nov. 20, had not been finally approved but that it probably would be without major change.

The Government has traditionally gone slow in contract compliance because it does not want interference with its procurement practices. Civil rights leaders doubt that the Nixon Administration; which has strong ties to the business community, will take bold steps in this direction.

Following are the Equal Employment Opportunity Commission's figures on Negro employment and union membership in 1967:

NEGROES IN BUILDING TRADES

Union	Membership Totals	Negro	Per Cent Negro
Asbestos workers	6,104	61	0.9
Boilermakers	23,946	934	3.9
Bricklayers	34,069	3,300	9.6
Carpenters	315,538	5,284	1.6
Electrical workers	133,904	915	0.6
Elevator constructors	6,728	33	0.4
Operating engineers	103,677	4,200	4.0
Iron workers	70,273	1,197	1.7
Laborers	266,243	81,457	30.5
Lathers	4,660	177	3.7
Marble, slate, stone polishers	4,355	387	8.8
Painters	66,714	2,498	3.7
Plasterers	28,182	3,917	14.0
Plumbers	147,862	320	0.2
Roofers	10,807	1,461	13.5
Sheet metal workers	34,867	92	0.2
Totals	**1,257,929**	**106,263**	**8.4**

NEGROES IN REFERRAL UNIONS

	Building Trades All Const.	Mech Trades	Non-building Trades
Albuquerque	1.3%	0.0%	5.9%
Atlanta	22.8%	0.1%	0.3%
Birmingham	16.3%	0.0%	unavailable
Chicago	3.5%	0.4%	15.8%
Cleveland	4.6%	0.4%	37.6%
Houston	18.1%	0.0%	40.9%
Kansas City	10.8%	0.0%	10.2%
Los Angeles	8.2%	0.5%	9.4%
Memphis	16.6%	0.9%	0.7%
New Orleans	21.7%	0.3%	18.7%
New York	12.3%	8.2%	17.9%
San Francisco	13.2%	4.5%	10.0%
Washington	10.7%	3.4%	40.5%
Detroit	14.7%	0.5%	4.3%
United States	8.4%	0.8%	12.0%

DEMOCRATIC PROGRAMS

The Administration is promoting means of putting more wealth into the hands of minorities while reducing to a minimum the structured urban and poverty programs instituted by the Democrats.

In that regard, informed sources said, it was likely that contract compliance might be utilized more than it has been in the past.

What the new order seeks are affirmative action agreements from employers in recruiting minority workers, with the proviso that minority members recruited "approximate or equal the ratio of minorities to the applicant population in each location." This could be significant in industries with predominantly white work forces.

Court decisions rendered under Title VII have been generally favorable to the minorities, assuring greater judicial enforcement.

Herbert Hill, labor secretary for the National Association for the Advancement of Colored People, estimated there were now in the courts about 250 lawsuits filed by the Justice Department or by private organizations against alleged discriminatory employment practices.

U.S. Judge Upholds Controversial Philadelphia Plan to Increase Hiring of Minorities in Building Industry

BY DONALD JANSON | MARCH 15, 1970

PHILADELPHIA, MARCH 14 — The controversial Philadelphia Plan to increase minority employment in construction trades has cleared its first court hurdle.

Federal District Judge Charles R. Weiner upheld its constitutionality yesterday and ruled that it did not violate the Civil Rights Act of 1964.

"It is fundamental," he said in the 22-page decision, "that civil rights without economic rights are mere shadows."

The plan, promulgated last year by the Department of Labor, requires contractors to make good-faith efforts to hire specified percentages of blacks in federally aided projects costing $500,000 or more.

The Contractors Association of Eastern Pennsylvania, in a suit filed Jan. 6, sought an injunction against the plan and a declaration that it was unconstitutional.

CONTRACTORS' PLEA

The contractors said the plan denied them equal protection of the laws because it was being applied only here. But in February, Secretary of Labor George P. Shultz announced that it would be extended to 18 other cities, including New York, unless those cities devised satisfactory plans of their own.

The main argument in opposition to the plan was that it required racial "quotas" in hiring. The Civil Rights Act of 1964 forbade this in order to protect nonwhite workers against low quotas set by some employers.

The Philadelphia Plan, when first tried under the Johnson Administration in 1967, set quotas that unions and contractors held to be discrimination in reverse. Under the Nixon Administration, the quotas become more flexible "goals" within percentage ranges and the only requirement was good-faith effort to meet the goals.

Elmer B. Staats, United States Controller General, said the plan still violated the Civil Rights Act and declared he would not approve payment to contractors using the plan.

In December, the Senate supported the Staats view, then reversed itself under pressure from the Administration and civil rights forces and joined the House in rejecting an appropriations bill amendment that would have killed the plan.

The contractors' test suit followed. Robert J. Bray Jr., attorney for the 80 contracting companies in the association, said today it had not been determined whether the decision would be appealed.

Judge Weiner said the plan did not violate the civil rights act because it "does not require the contractor to hire a definite percentage of a minority group."

The plan's ground rules for Philadelphia, where more than a third of the population is black, call for contractors to pledge to try to hire blacks at a rate of at least 4 per cent of their employees for projects undertaken this year, 9 per cent next year, 14 in 1972 and a top range of 19 to 26 per cent after that. Some of the trade unions involved have no more than 1 per cent now and have long excluded Negroes.

Judge Weiner noted that the contractor was required only to "make every good faith effort" to achieve specified percentages. The Government has said that tests of this would include whether a contractor relied solely on unions to assign workers to him or, if necessary, participated in federally funded training programs and went to community organizations that had agreed to supply blacks.

The Philadelphia Plan has not gotten off the ground here, in large part because of the dispute over its legality.

"It is beyond question," Judge Weiner said, "that present employment practices have fostered and perpetuated a system that has effectively maintained a segregated class. That concept, if I may use the strong language it deserves, is repugnant, unworthy and contrary to present national policy."

He said the Philadelphia Plan would provide "an unpolluted breath of fresh air to ventilate this unpalatable situation."

The Stakes in Bakke

OPINION | BY ANTHONY LEWIS | SEPT. 12, 1977

BOSTON, SEPT. 11 — The construction industry in Massachusetts, as in much of the country, has "a long history of discrimination." So the United States Court of Appeals here said in 1974. Because generalized attempts to break down racial barriers had not worked, the court allowed the state to write into a building contract a goal of 20 percent minority workers.

Specific contract provisions of that kind — and less formal pressures by big private institutions such as universities — have begun to open the building business to minorities here in recent years. Not just carpenters but small contracting firms owned by blacks have got a foothold.

"You see a definite change when you go into the black community to discuss these things," said Robert Kiley, chairman of the authority that runs metropolitan Boston's big public transit system. "There is a new professional class — a business class, of people who want to make money and are making it.

"Sure, there has been an element of coercion. But it is working."

Mr. Kiley, who was deputy mayor of Boston before he took the transit job, is one of the most respected urban managers around these days. He is a tough-minded man, highly practical in dealing with the interests and pressures of the city. Right now he is worried about something that seems far away but that he thinks could have a damaging effect on his business and more broadly on urban society: a case to be argued next month in the Supreme Court.

It is the case of Allan Bakke, the white Californian who says he was unconstitutionally refused admission to medical school because places were reserved for minority students. What worries Robert Kiley is the possibility that a decision in favor of Mr. Bakke could undo the effective efforts at encouraging minority business in the Massachusetts construction industry.

The concern is not just a general one but relates to a current project of Mr. Kiley's authority. One of Boston's main subway lines is being relocated. Because the project runs through an area where much of the city's minority population is concentrated, the authority decided to make it a target for minority participation.

Last spring the authority asked for bids on a $20 million subway tunnel. It wrote into the contract a provision that the successful bidder make "every reasonable effort" to have 30 percent of his subcontractors be minority controlled businesses qualified to do the work. The Federal Department of Transportation, which is aiding the project, approved the clause.

The low bidder was a big local builder, the Perini Corporation. But Perini scheduled only 13 percent of the work for what it termed minority contractors, and the main one of those was found by the transit authority to be not really controlled by minority persons. The authority awarded the contract to another company, which more than met the 30 percent target.

Perini sued, claiming in Federal Court that the contract provision was an unconstitutional "preference based on race." The suit sought an injunction against the authority, forbidding it to proceed on the project with the successful bidder.

After one brief restraining order to consider the arguments, the court has allowed the project to go ahead. But the case is due to be tried next month, on Perini's claim for a permanent injunction or damages.

If Perini wins, that would be the end of the authority's program for black and other minority contractors, who before now have been given virtually no work by the transit system. And the present program is a pretty modest one: If this disputed tunnel contract goes ahead exactly as planned, only 6 percent of the authority's entire 1977 construction work will have gone to minority firms.

Anyone who hopes for a color-blind society may be troubled by a program to give a specific share of public contracts to particular minorities. But right now it is a, perhaps the, effective way to break a historic pattern of discrimination. The reality is that it takes heroic measures to end the exclusion of blacks from certain areas of American life — not only in Massachusetts and not only in the construction business.

The Massachusetts example indicates why so much may be riding on the outcome of the Bakke case. Lawyers will find differences between the reservation of places at a medical school and the setting of goals for minority contractors. The reasons for the policy are clearer in the transit authority's evidence than in the rather scant record of the Bakke case. But what the Supreme Court says could still be decisive.

Black leaders and members of Congress have lately been pressing President Carter to do more for minority employment and support the Humphrey-Hawkins Bill. But any such action would be trivial in its effect compared to the impact of a Supreme Court decision sharply limiting efforts to bring minorities into the mainstream of American society.

ANTHONY LEWIS is an Op-Ed columnist for The New York Times.

N.A.A.C.P. Says Bakke Ruling Has Brought Cuts in Minority Plans

BY THOMAS A. JOHNSON | JAN. 9, 1979

THE NATIONAL ASSOCIATION for the Advancement of Colored People charged yesterday that "the plurality of opinions in the Bakke case" has led some educational institutions in the United States "to commence tampering with and, in some instances, boldly uprooting, special programs aimed at assisting minorities."

The charges were made in the annual report of the association's legal department and amount to the first evaluation by a civil rights organization of the effects of the United States Supreme Court's decision in the case.

In June, the Court invalidated the admissions program at the medical school of the University of California at Davis because it set aside 16 places in each freshman class for minority-group members and ordered the admission of Allan P. Bakke. But the Court also upheld the constitutionality of other school plans that use racial or ethnic background as a factor in determining admissions.

REPORT AT NATIONAL MEETING

Written by the association's general counsel, Nathaniel R. Jones, the report was presented on the last day of the association's three-day national board meeting at the New York Sheraton Hotel.

Mr. Jones also said that employers are known to be using the decision to "justify eliminating or cutting back on affirmative hiring and promotional programs." He added that "institutions and employers who have affirmative-action programs have become the targets of so called 'reverse discrimination' suits."

And at a news conference, the 70-year-old organization's executive director, Benjamin L. Hooks, said that the months since the decision had been "more disturbing than we thought they would be." The

BETTMANN/GETTY IMAGES

Demonstrators, protesting a California court decision in the Bakke case, rallying at an Oakland park, Oct. 8, 1977. The case worked through the lower courts before reaching the Supreme Court, sparking multiple protests over the course of its review.

Court's decision, he said, has had "far more chilling impact that we thought it would have."

Spokesmen for Rutgers, Yale and the University of Pennsylvania, which Mr. Jones identified by name as being among the "many" that had "tampered with" or "uprooted" affirmative-action programs, denied the N.A.A.C.P. charges.

YALE PROCEDURES 'MODIFIED'

Harry Wellington, dean of the Yale Law School, said that Yale had "modified some procedures" but that it had not changed its commitment to admit members of minority groups. The modification, he said, was to stop considering minority applications "separate and apart from other applications."

The associate dean of Rutgers University Law School in Newark said that a "large majority of the faculty decided to retain the concept of the 10-year-old special admissions program and expand its size to 30 percent of the entering class and to open it to all applicants of disadvantaged backgrounds." He said that the action placed the program on "a strong legal and ethical foundation." Formerly, the program encompassed 25 percent of the entering class.

Arnold Miller, the dean of admissions at the University of Pennsylvania Law School said that the school changed its policy of judging minorities as "special" to "correspond with the essence of the Bakke case."

Mr. Hooks and Mr. Jones said that another result of the Bakke decision was a plethora of actions by organizations representing white policemen and firemen, seeking to eliminate affirmative-action programs previously adopted by such cities as San Francisco, Detroit, Atlanta and Dayton.

Mr. Jones also said that the N.A.A.C.P. would file a brief in support of the affirmative action plan now under attack at a Kaiser Aluminum and Chemical Corporation plant in Louisiana.

In the case, a white employee, Brian F. Weber, contends that the program, administered by Kaiser and the United Steelworkers of America, discriminates against him because he is white. Mr. Weber has been upheld by two Federal courts. The Supreme Court has agreed to hear the matter.

Affirmative Action Ruling Is Called a Breakthrough

ANALYSIS | BY LINDA GREENHOUSE | JULY 4, 1980

WASHINGTON, JULY 3 — Even read narrowly, yesterday's Supreme Court decision upholding a Congressionally enacted affirmative action program was a breakthrough. For the first time the Court explicitly endorsed the power of Congress to award Federal benefits on the basis of race.

But the Court's acceptance of the essential premise of affirmative action is so clear in the two majority opinions that the decision is unlikely to remain confined to the Congressional arena.

Coming two years after the ambiguous opinions in the Bakke case, and one year after the carefully confined statutory ruling in the Weber case, yesterday's decision gives renewed legal and political momentum to affirmative action at all levels of government. Despite its cautious tone, Fullilove v. Klutznick is a powerful constitutional statement likely to become a potent tool for racial minorities seeking, in the words of Chief Justice Warren E. Burger, "to achieve the goal of equality of economic opportunity."

BASIC PREMISE DEFINED

The premise that the six Justices in the majority accepted was this: Not only does the Constitution not require strict color-blindness in the pursuit of that goal, but also color-blindness is inadequate when disadvantaged groups have to catch up to compete.

In upholding a public works program that entitled a sizable list of minorities to 10 percent of Federal construction grants, the Court said that Congress had the authority to identify the problem to be remedied, design the remedy, identify the recipients and place the nonrecipients at a disadvantage.

"The Court has crossed a Rubicon," Paul Mishkin, a law professor at the University of California, said today. Professor Mishkin wrote the brief defending the affirmative action program that the Supreme Court struck down in the Bakke decision. "Whether a state, as opposed to Congress, can set up a remedial system is a somewhat distinct question," he continued, "but it's a distinction that won't stand up."

The Bakke case concerned the validity of a special admissions program for members of minorities at a state medical school. While the Court struck down the specific program, it held that race could constitutionally be taken into account in an appropriately tailored program based on adequate findings of past discrimination.

But the implications of Bakke remained obscure. After yesterday, it is Bakke's importance that seems shadowy. "Bakke doesn't mean much now," Eric Schnapper, a lawyer for the N.A.A.C.P. Legal Defense and Educational Fund Inc., said today. "I think Fullilove ultimately covers just about every affirmative action approach around today."

But some of the hardest questions raised by those approaches are yet to be answered. By accepting two new cases yesterday for argument and decision in the new term that begins in October, the Justices indicated that some of the answers would not be long in coming.

Among the questions left hanging by the decisions of the last few terms are these:

• Assuming that a race-based remedy for discrimination is permissible, how should the remedy be designed? What is a valid "target?" If a 10 percent set-aside is acceptable, what about 30 percent?

• Is it constitutional to take away someone's vested right or legitimate expectation in the name of creating new opportunity for someone else?

• When does a policy that distinguishes among racial groups for the purpose of a "benign" remedy cross the barrier and become invidious, and therefore unconstitutional, racial discrimination?

In its broad deference to Congress, the majority in Fullilove paid scant attention to the 10 percent figure. Last year's Weber decision, which upheld the legality under the Civil Rights Act of 1964 of an affirmative action program in the steel industry, failed to address the harder issues for two reasons. First, the Court treated the plan as purely voluntary, and in the absence of "state action" there was no occasion to reach the constitutional issue. And second, the affirmative action goal in Weber was accomplished through an entirely new training program that did not take from white workers a benefit they previously enjoyed.

One of the cases the Court accepted yesterday for review is a challenge to an affirmative action program in the California prison system, which presents the "state action" absent in Weber. The program set a goal for the hiring of corrections officers of 38 percent women and 35 percent racial minorities. Two white male officers sued on the ground that they had lost opportunities for promotion.

The second case tests the outer limits of the benign remedy. The Chicago school board, in the name of "stabilizing" transitional neighborhoods, turned black students away from two local high schools to preserve a 50-50 racial balance. The blacks sued, and two Federal courts said that the plan was a justified tool for maintaining integration.

These cases pose questions without obvious "right" answers. The Court demonstrated yesterday that it is unafraid of the questions and willing to look for creative solutions.

Plans to Ease Hiring Rules Attacked

BY COLIN CAMPBELL | AUG. 26, 1981

CIVIL RIGHTS AND women's groups reacted angrily yesterday to the Reagan Administration's decision to ease Federal rules that require companies doing business with the Government to file plans for taking affirmative action to hire women and members of minority groups.

"They're doing this now," said Benjamin L. Hooks, executive director of the National Association for the Advancement of Colored People, "and next week it will be something else. It's like water on a rock. Someday it will chop a hole in the hopes of black people."

Eleanor Smeal, president of the National Organization for Women, said, "This is another major setback under the Reagan Administration for equality for women."

BUSINESS GROUP'S VIEW

The United States Chamber of Commerce, however, maintained that the Administration's proposed changes did not go far enough. "Businesses will still have to deal with tons of paperwork," said John P. Brandenburg, a labor law specialist for the business lobbyist group.

The Labor Department's proposals would require the filing of formal documents outlining minority hiring and recruitment plans only from Federal contractors with 250 or more employees and with contracts worth more than $1 million. The existing rules apply to companies of 50 or more employees and to contracts over $50,000.

The proposals, which affect regulations that cover 30 million workers and 200,000 companies that provide goods and services to the Federal Government, were published yesterday in the Federal Register. A final version of the new rules will be published after 60 days and will go into effect a month after that.

The Reagan Administration has promised to cut or simplify regulations in order to stem the growth of Government, reduce paperwork for businesses and lower the costs of doing business.

"The only thing it's doing," said Mr. Brandenburg of the Chamber of Commerce, "is taking a very, very bad program, tinkering with it a little bit, and saying that it's not going to apply to as many people as before. That's not getting to the guts of the problem."

PLAN IS ATTACKED

Several spokesmen for black civil rights groups asserted that the new regulations would permit 75 percent of Government contractors, including the important construction industry, to avoid observing laws against discrimination in hiring. To argue, as the Labor Department did yesterday, that easing the affirmative-action rules "will create incentive or voluntary compliance" was "Orwellian doubletalk," Mr. Hooks said.

He made the comments in an interview after the monthly meeting in New York of the Black Leadership Forum, a group of 16 civil rights leaders.

The meeting of the Black Leadership Forum, of which Mr. Hooks is chairman, was also attended by Joseph E. Lowery, president of the Southern Christian Leadership Conference; Representative Walter E. Fauntroy, chairman of the Congressional Black Caucus; M. Carl Holman, president of the National Urban Coalition; Dorothy I. Height, national president of the National Council of Negro Women, and about half a dozen other black leaders.

Mr. Hooks, when asked what effect the Administration's proposals might have on the morale of American blacks, who recent public opinion polls have indicated are becoming increasingly gloomy about the future of the nation and blacks, said: "We were saying before the polls came out that the Reagan Administration wasn't friendly to black people, but we were told to shut up and sit in a corner."

OTHER PROVISIONS OF RULES

The Administration's proposed new rules, in addition to easing the filing requirements for small Government contractors, would also simplify the rules for contractors with 250 to 499 employees. The proposed rules would exempt contractors from taking remedial action if the number of women and members of minority groups employed by them reached 80 percent of the figures deemed appropriate under current formulas.

Donna Lenhoff, a lawyer with the Women's Legal Defense Fund, said: "This is not a cutback on recordkeeping. It is a cutback on justice." Other women's groups made similar statements. None seemed especially surprised at the Administration's action.

Several critics of the action, including Ray Marshall, who was Secretary of Labor under President Carter, said they thought it was a mistake to exempt small concerns because they accounted for most of the nation's jobs, particularly new jobs.

Mr. Brandenburg of the Chamber of Commerce, on the other hand, said that businesses had already made great strides in complying with Federal hiring laws.

Rights Panel Sees Decline in U.S. Enforcement

BY JULIE JOHNSON | JAN. 18, 1989

WASHINGTON, JAN. 17 — A private commission today reported a "dramatic decline" in civil rights enforcement by the Federal Government under the Reagan Administration and urged that President-elect George Bush appoint a Cabinet-level group "to deal with the causes and results of bigotry and prejudice."

The call by the 17-member Citizens Commission on Civil Rights came a day after Mr. Bush hailed the Rev. Dr. Martin Luther King Jr. as a hero and pledged to be more responsive to concerns of black Americans.

Such attempts by Mr. Bush and Republican Party officials to broaden their appeal to blacks and other minorities drew praise from Arthur S. Flemming, the panel's chairman, who was dismissed by President Reagan in November 1981 as the chairman of the United States Commission on Civil Rights because of his strong advocacy of busing and affirmative action.

Mr. Flemming, a moderate Republican whose public service dates from the Eisenhower Administration, said in an interview that the President-elect's actions were "positive" and harked back to a "pre-1980 Bush."

Among the findings in the panel's report, "One Nation, Indivisible: The Civil Rights Agenda for the 1990s," to be published in March, members concluded that a pattern of persistent discrimination and lack of enforcement exists in housing, voting rights, education and employment.

The commission, which released a prepublication summary today, cited these examples:

• The Justice Department since 1981 has filed only 31 cases challenging discriminatory voting practices and 15 cases to enforce the Voting Rights Act.

• While the Department of Housing and Urban Development estimates that 2 million instances of housing discrimination occur annually, an average of only 10 new fair housing cases have been filed each year since 1981.

• In 1987 the median income for black families was $18,098, a drop of nearly $1,000 from the income median for black families in 1978.

Mark Weaver, a Justice Department spokesman, characterized as "nonsense" the implication that the Government's civil rights lawyers had light caseloads.

Asserting that the department had filed at least 500 objections to voting changes made by the states, largely in the South, Mr. Weaver said the civil rights section "is probably one of the busiest."

He also said the commission was "ignoring" the fact that the Justice Department in the Reagan years had won a major housing discrimination case in Yonkers, N.Y., that a voting rights case was pending in Los Angeles County and that a discrimination case was filed to ban hiring bias in the New Jersey police recruiting system. The case in Yonkers was filed by the department in the Carter Administration.

William L. Taylor, a member of the citizens' commission and the former staff director of the United States Civil Rights Commission, said the nation's civil rights climate has been "very depressed over the last several years."

Bush Vows Rights Effort on Jobs and Economic Development

BY JULIE JOHNSON | AUG. 9, 1989

WASHINGTON, AUG. 8 — President Bush renewed the Administration's commitment to equal opportunity today, pledging to rebuild the nation's urban areas by focusing on education, job training and economic development.

"I want to make sure everyone in this room knows just where I stand, just where my Administration stands," Mr. Bush told the annual conference of the National Urban League here. "My Administration is committed to reaching out to minorities, to striking down barriers to free and open access. We will not tolerate discrimination, bigotry or bias of any kind, period."

Mr. Bush used his appearance, the first by a President before the group since 1977, to continue White House efforts to build support among black Americans and civil rights groups, who were frequently at odds with Ronald Reagan's Administration and who have clashed in recent months with Mr. Bush's.

"Your problems are my problems," the President said. "Today, I offer you my hand. I offer you my word. Together, we will make American open and equal to all."

TOUCHY ISSUES AVOIDED

But Mr. Bush avoided mention of issues that have recently angered civil rights groups, like the Supreme Court rulings that they said narrowed anti-discrimination laws, or his nomination of William C. Lucas to be head of the Justice Department's civil rights division, a choice that was rejected by the Senate Judiciary Committee.

Mr. Lucas, a black former Executive of Wayne County, Mich., was criticized as lacking the legal experience needed to be the nation's top civil rights enforcement official.

Mr. Bush has won high marks from civil rights groups for embracing affirmative action and working behind the scenes on legislation like amendments to the Fair Housing Act and the Americans with Disabilities Act.

LEAGUE FOCUSES ON BUSINESS

Weighing against Mr. Bush among some civil rights leaders is his refusal when he was Vice President to criticize President Reagan on his actions on civil rights issues, like his veto of the Civil Rights Restoration Act. That measure was in response to a 1984 Supreme Court decision limiting the scope of anti-discrimination provisions connected with the use of Federal money. Congress later overrode Mr. Reagan's March 1988 veto.

Today, Mr. Bush was received warmly by the Urban League members, who interrupted his speech with applause several times. He tailored his remarks to the league, a civil rights organization that works closely with businesses and focuses on employment and economic development.

Repeating his support for tax incentives to encourage business enterprises to locate in the inner cities, Mr. Bush said, "The future of urban America depends on bringing growth to our inner cities."

John E. Jacob, the league's president, praised Mr. Bush for language that he said sets a new tone for the nation on civil rights, and he said the President's positions on education and drugs were in line with those of the Urban League.

"What we heard from him today is that he has said his Administration will do everything within its power to make sure that discrimination does not exist in this country and that they will fight it with every weapon that they have," Mr. Jacob said. "I think that's important because this nation needs to have not only a reordering of its priorities but a reordering of the nation's atmosphere, to move the nation back toward the center."

SPEECH SEEN AS LACKING SPECIFICS

But Clarence L. Barney, the New Orleans Urban League president, who is chairman of the national group's economic development committee, said Mr. Bush had to be assessed by his policies.

"Though I was very impressed with the tone, style and sincerity of the President's speech, I would like to have seen a greater degree of specificity," he said.

He praised Mr. Bush's comment that the nation must "create conditions for urban growth and economic revival." But Mr. Barney said it was unrealistic for black contractors to focus solely on inner cities with hopes of building "economic wealth out of poverty."

Mr. Barney said black business leaders "want to rebuild our inner-city neighborhoods, but we don't want to be consigned or restricted to that," adding, "The greatest opportunities are in foreign investment and in rebuilding our infrastructure." It is estimated that $1.4 trillion will have to be spent in coming years rebuilding the nation's deteriorating highways, waterways and other public structures.

APPEARANCE WAS MONITORED

Several civil rights organizations and Administration officials, particularly those who have been involved in skirmishes with the Bush White House, closely monitored Mr. Bush's appearance at the Urban League meeting, which concludes Wednesday.

Ralph Neas, executive director of the Leadership Conference on Civil Rights, a coalition of several groups that helped marshal opposition to the nomination of Mr. Lucas, said, "Everyone in the civil rights community applauds the new tone that President Bush has set, and this speech is another indication of that tone."

But despite the oratory, Mr. Neas said, many groups in his coalition are "deeply disappointed" that Mr. Bush sees no need for the proposed legislation to counteract Supreme Court rulings that made it harder to bring and win suits charging discrimination.

William Barclay Allen, chairman of the Civil Rights Commission, said in an interview after reading a text of the President's remarks: "It's nice to have this statement. These are very important problems, but we must also recognize that civil rights is bigger."

Justices, 5 to 4, Cast Doubts on U.S. Programs That Give Preferences Based on Race

BY LINDA GREENHOUSE | JUNE 13, 1995

WASHINGTON, JUNE 12 — In a decision likely to fuel rather than resolve the debate over affirmative action, the Supreme Court today cast doubt on the constitutionality of Federal programs that award benefits on the basis of race.

Federal programs that classify people by race, even for an ostensibly benign purpose such as expanding opportunities for members of minorities, are presumably unconstitutional, the Court said in a 5-to-4 opinion. Writing for the majority, Justice Sandra Day O'Connor said such programs must be subject to the most searching judicial inquiry and can survive only if they are "narrowly tailored" to accomplish a "compelling governmental interest."

This formidable standard is one that the Court has applied to state affirmative action programs since 1989, when it invalidated a public works program in Richmond in which 30 percent of all contracts had to be set aside for companies owned by members of minorities. The decision today marked an important doctrinal shift for the Court, which until now had given the Federal Government significantly more leeway for its affirmative action efforts. The constitutional guarantee of equal protection should mean the same at all levels of government, Justice O'Connor said.

While the standard the Court adopted today has historically been very difficult to meet, the Court stopped short of declaring unconstitutional either the particular Federal construction program before it today or Federal affirmative action in general.

The Court's ruling was greeted with enthusiasm by some conservatives, who saw it as the beginning of the end of the era of affirmative action. Supporters of affirmative action, however, while acknowledging the decision as a setback, declined to see it as a disaster.

Justice O'Connor's opinion included an important qualification, leaving the door open to the defense of such programs in future cases. "We wish to dispel the notion that strict scrutiny is 'strict in theory, but fatal in fact,' " Justice O'Connor said, quoting from an opinion of the late Justice Thurgood Marshall. She continued: "The unhappy persistence of both the practice and the lingering effects of racial discrimination against minorities in this country is an unfortunate reality, and government is not disqualified from acting in response to it."

Two members of the majority, Justices Antonin Scalia and Clarence Thomas, would have gone considerably further and ruled that affirmative action can never be justified. "Under our Constitution there can be no such thing as either a creditor or a debtor race," Justice Scalia said.

Justice Thomas said: "In my mind, government-sponsored racial discrimination based on benign prejudice is just as noxious as discrimination inspired by malicious prejudice. In each instance, it is racial discrimination, plain and simple."

In declining to adopt those categorical views, the majority opinion, which Chief Justice William H. Rehnquist and Justice Anthony M. Kennedy also joined, left numerous issues to be resolved in future cases. These include the fate of the preference program at issue today, which provides a financial bonus to contractors on Federal highway programs who subcontract part of the work to businesses owned by "socially and economically disadvantaged individuals." The presumption under the law is that blacks and members of other minorities meet that definition, although the presumption may be rebutted in individual cases and white contractors may seek to qualify as "disadvantaged."

The case today was brought by a white contractor who lost a job to a Hispanic-owned company that had submitted a higher bid for a subcontract to build guardrails on a Federal highway in Colorado. Both the Federal District Court in Denver and the United States Court of Appeals for the 10th Circuit, also in Denver, evaluated the program under the relaxed standard the Supreme Court had applied in earlier decisions and upheld it. The lower courts must now re-evaluate the program under the exacting standard the Court set today.

The decision today overturned the most recent of the Supreme Court's Federal affirmative action precedents, a 1990 decision called Metro Broadcasting v. F.C.C. that had upheld a Federal affirmative action program designed to increase the number of broadcast licenses awarded to members of minorities. Today's ruling also cast grave doubt on the continued validity of a 1980 decision, Fullilove v. Klutznick, that had sustained a Federal public works program that set aside 10 pecent of the value of contracts for businesses owned by blacks and other minorities.

Despite the qualifications and unanswered questions in the majority opinion, Justice O'Connor's tone was forceful. The two-tiered approach that subjected Federal affirmative action programs to more relaxed judicial review than those of the states was inconsistent with the "basic principle" that the Constitution's guarantees of equal protection "protect persons, not groups," Justice O'Connor said.

"All governmental action based on race," no matter by what level of government or for what purpose, must be subject to the most searching judicial scrutiny, she said, adding: "Whenever the government treats any person unequally because of his or her race, that person has suffered an injury that falls squarely within the language and spirit of the Constitution's guarantee of equal protection."

The decision, Adarand Constructors v. Peña, No. 93-1841, is certain to encourage legal challenges to a range of Federal affirmative action programs. At the same time, the issue is being vigorously debated in Congress and in the White House, with the Clinton Administration now in the midst of a sweeping review of Federal racial preference programs. By refusing to foreclose affirmative action as a constitutional option, the Court has done little to relieve President Clinton, as well as other elected officials now confronting the issue, of the need to make and defend their own policy choices.

Affirmative action is also the subject of vigorous debate in the states. Last month, Gov. Pete Wilson of California ordered an end to all state affirmative action programs not required by law or by a court decree. Next year, Californians will vote on a ballot initiative to end affirmative action in state hiring and higher education.

Justice O'Connor's opinion did not precisely define the essential terms, "narrowly tailored" and "compelling interest," by which courts are to judge whether a challenged affirmative action survives the required "strict scrutiny." The opinion referred only to definitions that "this Court has set out in previous cases."

The terms are familiar in the jargon-filled discourse of equal protection, however. In earlier cases, the Court has insisted on evidence rather than generalized assertions about the history of racial discrimination to be overcome. The Court has also asked whether equivalently helpful results could have been achieved through alternative programs that did not classify people by race, and has sought evidence that the program will not last indefinitely.

There were three dissenting opinions today, filed by Justices John Paul Stevens, David H. Souter and Ruth Bader Ginsburg. Justice Stephen G. Breyer, who also dissented, joined Justices Souter's and Ginsburg's opinions.

The position of Justice Stevens was perhaps the most interesting on the Court, because he was a dissenter from the 1980 decision that upheld the Federal public works set-aside program. Justice O'Connor, who was not on the Court in 1980, quoted at length in her majority opinion today from Justice Stevens's dissent, in which he said that the racial classifications the Court upheld in the Fullilove case "can only exacerbate rather than reduce racial prejudice" and "will delay the time when race will become a truly irrelevant, or at least insignificant, factor."

It is a measure of the Court's shift to the right in the intervening 15 years, and of the 75-year-old Justice's consequent journey from the Court's center to its liberal wing, that found Justice Stevens in dissent today, calling for adherence to precedent. If the rigidly race-conscious program the Court upheld in 1980 was constitutional, he said, "it must follow as night follows the day" that the more flexible program at issue today was constitutional as well.

Justice Stevens also voted with the majority in the 1989 decision, City of Richmond v. Croson, that held that state and local affirmative action programs must be subject to strict judicial scrutiny. Today, he said there were important reasons for Federal programs to receive more deference from the Court. "Federal affirmative-action programs represent the will of our entire Nation's elected representatives," he said, "whereas a state or local program may have an impact on non-resident entities who played no part in the decision to enact it."

Justice Stevens said that the majority today had overlooked the difference between invidious discrimination and efforts to "foster equality in society" through race-based preferences. "There is no moral or constitutional equivalence between a policy that is designed to perpetuate a caste system and one that seeks to eradicate racial subordination," he said.

Justice Stevens said the Court's search for "consistency" on racial classifications "would treat a Dixiecrat Senator's decision to vote against Thurgood Marshall's confirmation in order to keep African Americans off the Supreme Court on a par with President Johnson's evaluation of his nominee's race as a positive factor."

Justice Souter, in his dissenting opinion, suggested that at the end of the day, Federal affirmative action programs might be upheld even under the majority's analysis. "Of course there will be some interpretive forks in the road before the significance of strict scrutiny for congressional remedial statutes becomes entirely clear," he said.

Administration Backs Affirmative Action Plan

BY NEIL A. LEWIS | AUG. 11, 2001

WASHINGTON, AUG. 10 — In its first opportunity to take a stance on affirmative action, the Bush administration asked the Supreme Court tonight to uphold a Transportation Department program intended to help minority contractors.

In a brief filed with the court, the Justice Department took the same position as the Clinton administration had in the case, which grew out of a challenge brought years ago by a white-owned construction company in Colorado Springs.

The company, Adarand Constructors, had submitted the low bid for a Transportation Department contract. But the contract was awarded to a minority contractor as part of the department's "disadvantaged business enterprise" program. Adarand sued, challenging the policy.

The case has become somewhat muddled since the Supreme Court first ruled on it in 1995. Then, by a 5-to-4 vote, the justices set strict limits on federal affirmative action programs, ruling that such programs must be narrowly tailored to meet a compelling government interest.

The court found that the program appeared flawed and should be reviewed by lower courts to see whether using race as a factor was justified in the award of federal contracts.

Last September, the United States Court of Appeals for the 10th Circuit, in Denver, said the program met the "strict scrutiny" test and was constitutional.

Moreover, since the Supreme Court's first ruling, the program has been sharply altered.

Under the revised program, even white-owned small businesses can apply for consideration as a disadvantaged business. In addition, the new version of the program no longer distributes financial bonuses to contractors that use minority-owned companies as subcontractors.

In January, during its last day in office, the Clinton administration argued that the program now met the Supreme Court's objections and that the court should decline to reopen the matter. When the justices voted in March to hear a renewed appeal by Adarand, the Bush administration faced its first significant test on affirmative action.

In its brief filed tonight, the Justice Department said that "the program is not unconstitutional."

The 50-page brief cited the program changes that let companies that are economically disadvantaged apply for the same preferences in receiving contracts. The department argued that the program was revised to minimize harm "to innocent third parties" and to create "as level a playing field as possible."

But the Bush administration brief also appears to accept an underlying tenet of affirmative action: that some businesses have suffered as a result of their minority ownership.

During the presidential campaign, George W. Bush said he opposed quotas but spoke of a need for "affirmative access," a stance that left his position on the issue ambiguous.

The decision today by the Bush administration was sharply criticized by traditional opponents of affirmative action. Linda Chavez, president of the Center for Equal Opportunity, a conservative group that studies affirmative action programs, said she was deeply disappointed.

"It's both bad policy and bad politics," said Ms. Chavez, who had been President Bush's choice for secretary of labor before she withdrew her nomination. "First of all, it's never good politics to betray your principles, and all the people involved in making this policy are people who have opposed racial preferences."

Attorney General John Ashcroft was one person Ms. Chavez cited. As a senator in 1998, Mr. Ashcroft voted against the program.

MARIO TAMA/STRINGER/AFP/GETTY IMAGES

Linda Chavez announcing her withdrawal from the nomination process for Secretary of Labor in January.

But Mindy Tucker, the Justice Department spokeswoman, said that "this is John Ashcroft doing what he said he would do in the confirmation process," noting that Mr. Ashcroft had pledged in his Senate testimony to defend even those laws with which he disagreed.

Georgina Verdugo, the executive director of Americans for a Fair Chance, a coalition of several major civil rights groups that advocates affirmative action, said she was pleasantly surprised by the Bush administration's approach.

"It's the administration's first real statement on affirmative action," she said. "This particular program has been through so many changes it is quite clear that it now meets the Supreme Court's requirements that it be better tailored as a remedy."

The case is to be heard by the Supreme Court sometime this fall.

Supreme Court Dismisses Challenge in Its Main Affirmative Action Case

BY LINDA GREENHOUSE | NOV. 28, 2001

WASHINGTON, NOV. 27 — The marquee affirmative action case of the Supreme Court's current term evaporated today when the justices dismissed a constitutional challenge to a federal highway contracting program and conceded that the case had been "improvidently granted."

The dismissal of Adarand Constructors v. Mineta, less than a month after argument, brought an ambiguous conclusion to a small Colorado subcontractor's long-running lawsuit over the federal government's effort to address the history of racial discrimination in the highway construction industry. In an unsigned seven-page opinion, the justices said that Adarand had not established its suitability as a plaintiff to challenge the one aspect of the federal program that they said was still before the court.

But the debate over affirmative action in general, and the federal government's role in particular, is not likely to be absent for long from the court's calendar. In lower federal courts around the country, there are a number of similar lawsuits pending that could provide the justices with a case without the flaws the Supreme Court found today in Adarand's appeal.

Beyond those cases, which deal with various aspects of the federal highway program, are other affirmative action cases in the pipeline, including a challenge to race-conscious assignments to public housing in Yonkers, which is now awaiting action by the justices, and an appeal to be argued before a federal appeals court next month on the constitutionality of affirmative action in admissions to the University of Michigan.

The court's action today had no general legal significance and, given the crowded affirmative action landscape, would have provided little more than a footnote to the term except for the symbolic importance the Adarand case has acquired during its years before the Supreme Court.

As Adarand Constructors v. Peña, the case led in 1995 to a landmark Supreme Court decision that for the first time applied to federal affirmative action programs the same "strict scrutiny" the court had earlier applied to state and local programs. Under this standard, adopted by a 5-to-4 vote, any race-conscious federal program had to serve a "compelling state interest" and be "narrowly tailored" to accomplish its goal.

At that time, Adarand, which is owned by a white family in Colorado Springs, was complaining that its constitutional right to equal protection was violated by an aspect of the federal highway program that gave contractors a financial bonus for awarding subcontracts to companies owned by members of minority groups. Despite having been the low bidder, Adarand lost a subcontract for making guardrails for a federal highway project.

In the first Adarand case, the court did not declare the bonus program unconstitutional, but rather ordered the lower federal courts to consider whether the program could meet the new test of strict scrutiny. After resolving various complications in the case, the United States Court of Appeals for the 10th Circuit, in Denver, ruled last year that the bonus, known as the subcontractor compensation clause, was unconstitutional.

However, the government by then had stopped using that clause, in an effort to address the Supreme Court's concerns and save the overall program from constitutional attack. New regulations were now in place that made the program constitutional, the 10th Circuit ruled.

Adarand appealed again to the Supreme Court last November, arguing that the program still incorporated racial preferences that failed the strict scrutiny test. In its closing days, the Clinton Administration told the justices not to take the new case. In a brief filed on Jan. 19 of this year, the Clinton Administration's solicitor general, Seth P. Waxman, said that changes in the program had made Adarand's appeal "somewhat divorced from the concrete context of an actual application." The question on which Adarand sought review "is not well presented by this case," the brief said.

The decision whether to hear the appeal or wait for a better case was evidently the subject of serious dispute within the court. Before granting the case on March 26, the justices considered the case in four consecutive weekly conferences and also sent to the 10th Circuit for the full record. The justices' deliberations in their conferences are private, so it is only a matter of conjecture that the conservative majority decided to ignore the Clinton administration's warnings and proceed with the case despite the uncertainties.

But the fate of Adarand's appeal was sealed four months later when the Bush administration, in a brief filed by its solicitor general, Theodore B. Olson, put the flaws in the case into even sharper focus. Adarand's suit "has outlived the program that provoked it," Mr. Olson wrote, a position he repeated when he urged the court in the argument last month to dismiss the case.

Mr. Olson argued that the only aspect of the program now properly before the court, one that encouraged considerations of race in direct federal contract procurement, could no longer be challenged by Adarand because the affirmative action component of the program had been suspended in Colorado — the only state where Adarand does business — and other states in which a federal study showed discrimination in contracting to be no longer a serious problem.

Adarand's lawyer, William Perry Pendley, president of the Mountain States Legal Foundation in Denver, did not hide his anger at the administration in an interview today.

"The government engaged in an all-out effort to confuse the court in an attempt to stop the court from deciding this case, and it succeeded," Mr. Pendley said. He said both his client and his organization, a conservative public-interest law firm, would look for other opportunities to challenge the program.

In a separate case today, the court ruled 5 to 4 that federal prisoners cannot bring federal lawsuits for constitutional violations against private companies that operate prisons or halfway houses under contract with the government.

The case, Correctional Services Corporation v. Malesko, No. 00-860, did not resolve the question of whether individual employees of such companies can be sued.

Chief Justice William H. Rehnquist wrote the opinion, which overturned a ruling by the United States Court of Appeals for the Second Circuit, in Manhattan. Justices Sandra Day O'Connor, Anthony M. Kennedy, Antonin Scalia and Clarence Thomas joined the opinion. Justice John Paul Stevens dissented in an opinion joined by Justices David H. Souter, Ruth Bader Ginsburg and Stephen G. Breyer.

CHAPTER 4

Affirmative Action in Academia

One of the most dynamic theaters for affirmative action is within academia. Higher education is, after all, intended to prepare individuals for productive and professional lives. However, schools historically discriminated against minorities or people of lower economic standing before affirmative action was deployed to level the playing field. Policies, practices, laws and court rulings shifted frequently, often mirroring the opinions of the masses and the position of the governing administration at the time. This chapter covers these trends, some of the more influential court cases, as well as methods academia uses to promote diversity in enrollment such as racial quotas.

Court to Weigh College Admission That Gives Minorities Preference

BY LESLEY OELSNER | FEB. 23, 1977

WASHINGTON, FEB. 22 — The Supreme Court agreed today to decide on the constitutionality of state university admission programs that give special preferences to blacks and other minority-group members, often to the disadvantage of better-qualified white applicants.

Advocates describe such programs as "affirmative action," justified on the ground that the action is necessary to compensate for the effects of past discrimination. But critics have come to label the idea as "reverse discrimination."

The issue is one of the most controversial and difficult in civil rights today. The Court's decision to consider it sets the stage for a landmark ruling — both on the permissibility of the preferential university admissions policies, and also, perhaps, on the broader issue of voluntary affirmative action programs in general.

CALIFORNIA PROGRAM VOIDED

The Court took up the issue at the request of the regents of the University of California, who asked the Court to review a California State Supreme Court decision last year that invalidated as unconstitutional a special admissions program at the university's medical school at Davis.

The California court issued the decision in a lawsuit brought by a white man, Allan Bakke, who had been denied admission to the medical school and who contended that the special program illegally discriminated against him on the basis of race.

In other action today, the Court declined to review — and thus left standing — the conviction of John D. Ehrlichman in the so-called "plumbers" case. Mr. Ehrlichman, once President Nixon's chief domestic affairs adviser, entered prison voluntarily last fall to begin serving his sentence of 20 months to five years but had continued his effort to overturn the conviction on appeal.

The Court also ruled that the Sixth Amendment's guarantee of the right to counsel in a criminal case does not necessarily mean that it is unconstitutional for someone who is secretly a Government informer to sit in on discussions between a defendant and the defendant's attorney. The ruling came on a 7-to-2 vote in a South Carolina case.

In an opinion by Justice Byron R. White, the Court said that if the informer did not communicate the information he got from the meeting to anyone else — if he did not report it to the prosecutor, for instance — there is no threat to the Sixth Amendment right. Justices Thurgood Marshall and William J. Brennan Jr. dissented.

The constitutionality of special admissions programs had been before the Court once before, in 1974, in a case in which a white student, Marco P. DeFunis Jr., challenged policies of the University of Washington Law School. The Justices ultimately announced they were not going to decide the issue, however, on the ground that it was moot, since Mr. DeFunis had since been admitted to the school and was about to graduate.

A number of organizations including some civil rights groups, asked the Supreme Court in recent weeks not to take the California case because they contended the record of the case was deficient and thus was not a good vehicle for deciding such an important issue.

Other persons and groups, however, including both advocates and opponents of racial admissions programs, had filed friend-of-the-court statements urging the Court to take the case.

Among them were the deans of the four law schools of the University of California. The deans contended, in effect, that if special admissions programs were ruled unconstitutional the result would be an almost total absence of minority group members in the schools.

"The movement of minority groups toward meaningful representation in the profession will virtually cease," the deans said.

On the other side was a brief filed on behalf of two organizations, the Committee on Academic Non-Discrimination and Integrity, and the Mid-America Legal Foundation, which oppose such programs. They urged the Court to take the case in order to decide the issue, saying that "reverse discrimination" in student admissions is rampant throughout the United States."

The regents and the University of California said in urging the Court to take the case that the issue had become even more urgent since the DeFunis case. Demand for places in professional schools is growing, the regents said, and some lower courts have begun addressing the issue, without arriving at any consensus.

"The question is perhaps the most important equal protection issue of the decade," the regents said. "It lies at the core of the country's commitment to real equality of opportunity for all of its citizens."

DECISION CALLED URGENT

Mr. Bakke, who is in his late 30's, had asked the Court not to review the case and thus, in effect, to permit him to begin medical school next fall, pursuant to the California court's ruling. Mr. Bakke was twice rejected for admission to the school but the state court ordered him admitted as part of its decision against the regents.

As things now stand, Mr. Bakke may not be admitted because Justice William H. Rehnquist issued a stay last November, postponing effect of the lower court decision, pending appeal.

The medical school was created in 1968; in the entering class, there were 50 students, including three Asians but no other minority-group members. Over the next two years, the school worked out a special admissions program, putting it into effect in 1970.

The intention, according to the regents, was "to compensate for the effects of societal discrimination on disadvantaged applicants of racial or ethnic minority groups status."

'ENHANCED DIVERSITY' SOUGHT

Among the objectives of the program were "enhanced diversity in the student body and the profession, elimination of historic barriers to medical careers for disadvantaged racial and ethnic minority groups, and increased aspiration for such careers on the part of members of those groups."

The special admissions program worked basically by easing the regular requirements in filling a certain number of openings per class — typically, 16 openings. However, according to the regents, all admitted under the program were still "fully qualified."

The program was used for disadvantaged members of racial and ethnic minorities. Disadvantaged nonminority group members went through the regular admissions program according to the regents so did minority group applicants with no history of disadvantage.

By the regents' count, almost no blacks or Chicanos were admitted at Davis by regular admissions from 1970 through 1974.

The case specifically involves only state universities. However one lawyer in the case said today that the Court's ruling was likely to affect most institutions of higher education ultimately.

Argument in the case will probably take place in the fall.

"Until recently, most attempts to overcome the effects of this heritage of racial discrimination have proven unavailing. In the past decade, however, the implementation of numerous 'affirmative action' programs, much like the program challenged in this case, have resulted in at least some degree of integration in many of our institutions."

The Dangers of Racial Quotas

OPINION | BY LARRY M. LAVINSKY | JUNE 15, 1977

THIS FALL, THE United States Supreme Court will pass upon one of the most controversial and divisive issues of this decade — the constitutionality of racially-based special-admissions programs.

Widely used by professional schools to increase the representation of blacks and certain other racial and ethnic minorities in their student bodies, the programs employ racial preference and quotas — the traditional engines of discrimination — as the vehicle for social progress.

The case before the Court, Regents of California v. Bakke, places the issue in stark perspective. A state medical school had established a special admissions program based upon fixed quota: 16 out of 100 places in each entering class were reserved exclusively for minority-group members. The California Supreme Court, noting that the qualifications of some specially admitted minority students were substantially lower than white applicants denied admission, declared the program unconstitutional.

A series of United States Supreme Court decisions over the last 40 years has established that it would be unconstitutional for state professional schools to exclude black applicants because of their race. Now, the Court must decide whether social objectives justify the exclusion of white applicants because of their race. The decision will be of historic significance in determining whether the twin ideals of equality of opportunity and equality under law, will continue to be viable.

A racial quota in special admissions, however well intentioned, is destructive of equal opportunity. Given the limited number of places to be filled, quotas diminish the opportunity to compete of those who do not belong to the preferred group. Whether rationalized as a remedy for past inequities or for present underrepresentation, the quota approach could only be sustained if the Constitution is construed as affording whites less protection against discrimination than racial minorities. In effect, those for whom equality was demanded would be made more equal than others.

The supporters of racially-based special admissions characterize the discrimination inherent in such programs as "benign," and therefore constitutionally unobjectionable.

They rely on cases such as the recent Supreme Court decision sanctioning racial quotas in redistricting under the Voting Rights Acts. However, the racially-based redistricting in that case deprived no group of fair representation and no individual of the right to vote on account of race. Any racial discrimination involved, therefore, was "benign" in the sense that it assisted minority groups without depriving anyone of a legally recognized right or benefit.

The same is not true of the racial admissions quota involved in the Bakke case. There, minority-group members were assisted by systematically excluding whites from competing for one-sixth of the places in each entering class of the medical school.

The need to increase educational opportunities for minority students is undeniably a social imperative. All people of good will would therefore welcome nondiscriminatory programs designed to achieve this result. The medical school's supporters argue, however, that there is no nondiscriminatory way to increase minority representation in professional schools and that without racially-based special admissions, minority enrollment would fall sharply.

For example, a friend-of-the-court brief filed in the Bakke case on behalf of the deans of four California law schools rejects the possibility of opening special admissions programs to economically and educationally disadvantaged applicants of all races on the ground that "disadvantaged white and Asian applicants would tend to overwhelm black and Chicano applicants." The brief argues that a disadvantageousness approach would require a much larger compromise of academic standards than the existing program.

Given the serious implications of such claims, one would expect them to be supported by a substantial body of experience. This, however, is not the case. A recent report on special admissions by one of the law schools candidly admits that "to the extent that law schools have special admissions programs of any substance, they operate along racial rather than economic or other lines." The report concludes that there is no real body of experience in dealing with a disadvantageousness approach.

Only after nondiscriminatory approaches to special admissions programs have been tried and proved inadequate might there be a moral or legal justification for resorting to admissions influenced by race. The stakes are far too high for a society trying to rid itself of racial discrimination to accept on faith the claim that the only way to achieve equality in the professions is by practising still more racial discrimination.

LARRY M. LAVINSKY is a New York lawyer and chairman of the national civil rights committee of the B'nai B'rith Anti-Defamation League.

Moving Beyond Affirmative Action

OPINION | BY THOMAS J. ESPENSHADE | OCT. 4, 2012

PRINCETON, N.J. — On Wednesday, the Supreme Court will hear oral arguments in Fisher v. University of Texas, the latest in a long line of conservative assaults on affirmative action that dates to the late 1970s. Nearly a decade has passed since the court, in Grutter v. Bollinger, approved the continued use of race as one factor in an individualized, "holistic" review of an applicant's qualifications for higher education. Now even such limited consideration of race is being challenged.

Abigail Fisher, who is white, graduated from a Texas public high school in 2008 and barely missed out on automatic admission to the University of Texas at Austin under the Texas Top 10 Percent Law. When she was later denied admission after an evaluation that considered a candidate's race, she sued, alleging racial discrimination.

Supporters of race-conscious affirmative action in higher education are not optimistic that it will survive. But they shouldn't despair. A Supreme Court ruling against the university might put ethnic and racial diversity on college campuses on a firmer footing for the long term. It would spur Americans who care about racial inequality to seek alternatives to affirmative action by addressing the deeply entrenched disadvantages that lower-income and minority children face from the beginning of life. Race-based affirmative action has been a woefully inadequate weapon in the arsenal against inequality. It treats the symptoms but not the root causes of an underlying social problem. It is limited to the more selective private and public colleges (those that accept fewer than half of all applicants), which together account for about 20 percent of all freshmen. By my estimate, between 10,000 and 15,000 black and Hispanic students enroll in selective colleges every year through race-conscious policies. This is about 1 percent of the entering freshman class nationwide and just 1 percent of all black and Hispanic 18-year-olds.

ANNA PARINI

Graduation rates are higher for all students, not just underrepresented minority students, at more selective colleges. The trade-off is that students who are admitted through affirmative action (and who often have weaker academic credentials than their peers) are more likely to graduate toward the bottom of their class. Analyzing data from eight elite colleges (five private, three public) from 1999 and 2003, my colleague Alexandria Walton Radford and I found that one-half of black students and one-third of Hispanic students graduated in the bottom 20 percent of their class.

We also found that self-segregation dilutes the educational benefits of diversity that proponents of affirmative action rightly prize. Only half of the students in our sample reported having a roommate or close friend of a different race (or a different Hispanic ethnicity) during college. Finally, when asked about their level of satisfaction with the academic and social aspects of their college years, upper-middle-class white students reported the greatest satisfaction and working-class black students the least.

To be clear, I believe that race-conscious affirmative action is necessary, and often beneficial — though I am not hopeful that the court will agree. Our study showed that eliminating it would reduce the number of black students by about 60 percent, and the number of Hispanic students by about one-third, at selective private schools. We also showed that there is no substitute policy, including preferences based on socioeconomic class, that would generate as much racial and ethnic diversity as affirmative action, given the large numbers of working-class non-Hispanic whites and Asians in the applicant pool.

Most important, our study found that without affirmative action, racial diversity could only be preserved if there were no racial differences in learned skills and knowledge or in college preparedness.

The racial and socioeconomic gap in academic performance is America's most pressing domestic issue. When they enter kindergarten, black children are about one year behind white children. When they graduate from high school, black teenagers are four years behind white teenagers.

Despite the No Child Left Behind law, the Race to the Top initiative and endless debate over K-12 school reforms — accountability, standards, smaller classes, more effective teachers, better pay, charter schools, extended day, yearlong schools — the performance gaps have persisted, especially at the later ages.

If affirmative action is abolished, selective colleges and universities will face a stark choice. They can try to manufacture diversity by giving more weight in admissions to those factors that are sometimes close substitutes for race — for example, having overcome disadvantage in a poor urban neighborhood. Or they can take a far bolder step: putting their endowments and influence behind a comprehensive effort to close the learning gap that starts at birth. Higher education has a responsibility for all of education. The job of those atop the academic pyramid is not over once they've enrolled a diverse freshman class.

We need more research into the impact of factors like diet and nutrition, the amount of time parents talk and read with their kids, exposure to electronic screen time, sleep routines and the way stress outside the home affects family life. But we already know that an expansion of early-childhood education is urgently needed, along with programs, like peer-to-peer mentoring, that help low-income families support their children's learning. The first few years of life are the most critical ones, when parental investments and early-childhood interventions have a higher payoff than at later ages, particularly for disadvantaged children. Economists have estimated that the net taxpayer benefit from converting a high school dropout to a high school graduate is $127,000.

However the court decides the Fisher case, affirmative action's days appear numbered. Seven states — Arizona, California, Florida, Michigan, Nebraska, New Hampshire and Washington — have banned racial preferences in college admissions. In 2003, in the Grutter decision, Justice Sandra Day O'Connor wrote that she expected such preferences to disappear within 25 years — by 2028. The children who would go off to college that year are already 2 years old.

THOMAS J. ESPENSHADE, a professor of sociology at Princeton, is a co-author of "No Longer Separate, Not Yet Equal: Race and Class in Elite College Admission and Campus Life."

Between the Lines of the Affirmative Action Opinion

BY JOHN SCHWARTZ | JUNE 24, 2013

IN FISHER V. UNIVERSITY of Texas, the justices sent a thorny affirmative action case concerning the university's program to achieve racial diversity back to the lower courts for further consideration under a tougher standard of review. Justice Anthony M. Kennedy wrote the majority opinion and was joined by six colleagues. Justice Ruth Bader Ginsburg filed the sole dissent, and Justices Antonin Scalia and Clarence Thomas wrote concurring opinions. Justice Elena Kagan did not take part in the decision, presumably because of her prior role as solicitor general. Key passages are highlighted below, with analysis of their meaning and significance.

OPINION OF THE COURT

Justice Kennedy explains here that while the courts might give consideration to a university's judgment in devising a plan to reach a racially diverse population, the effects of that plan do not receive the same deference and must be proved to be "narrowly tailored" to the goal — and that it is up to the courts to ensure that a program does not make race or ethnicity "the defining feature" of the application.

> *Strict scrutiny does not permit a court to accept a school's assertion that its admissions process uses race in a permissible way without closely examining how the process works in practice, yet that is what the District Court and Fifth Circuit did here.*

Justice Kennedy is saying that the appeals court was too deferential to the university and its efforts to bring a "critical mass" of minority enrollment and should have applied tough standards of constitutional review outlined in two prior decisions, Grutter v. Bollinger and University of California v. Bakke.

The Court concludes that the Court of Appeals did not hold the University to the demanding burden of strict scrutiny articulated in Grutter and Regents of Univ. of Cal. v. Bakke ... Because the Court of Appeals did not apply the correct standard of strict scrutiny, its decision affirming the District Court's grant of summary judgment to the University was incorrect. That decision is vacated, and the case is remanded for further proceedings.

The Supreme Court ruled that the appeals court decision was in error, but that it would be unfair for it to overturn Texas' program. Instead, the justices sent the decision back to the lower courts for additional review, using the tough standard of strict scrutiny outlined in Justice Kennedy's opinion.

The District Court and Court of Appeals confined the strict scrutiny inquiry in too narrow a way by deferring to the University's good faith in its use of racial classifications and affirming the grant of summary judgment on that basis. The Court vacates that judgment, but fairness to the litigants and the courts that heard the case requires that it be remanded so that the admissions process can be considered and judged under a correct analysis.

Justice Kennedy, in closing his opinion, tries to make it clear that the requirement of strict scrutiny not be taken as a death knell for the Texas plan or any other university's efforts to pursue racial diversity as a goal in admissions.

Strict scrutiny must not be " 'strict in theory, but fatal in fact' ". ... But the opposite is also true. Strict scrutiny must not be strict in theory but feeble in fact.

CONCURRING OPINION BY JUSTICE SCALIA

Justice Scalia signals here that he would vote to overturn any racial preferences, in education or elsewhere.

I adhere to the view I expressed in Grutter v. Bollinger: 'The Constitution proscribes government discrimination on the basis of race, and state-provided education is no exception.'

CONCURRING OPINION BY JUSTICE THOMAS

Justice Thomas equates those seeking racial diversity to those upholding the cruelties of slavery, stating that "racial discrimination is never benign."

> *The University's professed good intentions cannot excuse its outright racial discrimination any more than such intentions justified the now denounced arguments of slaveholders and segregationists.*

Justice Thomas says that he voted with the majority because he agreed that the lower court had not properly applied the strict scrutiny standard from earlier cases. But, he added, he would have overruled an earlier affirmative action case, Grutter v. Bollinger, and its support for racial preference in admissions because of the "insidious consequences" of the preferences.

> *While it does not, for constitutional purposes, matter whether the University's racial discrimination is benign, I note that racial engineering does in fact have insidious consequences. There can be no doubt that the University's discrimination injures white and Asian applicants who are denied admission because of their race. But I believe the injury to those admitted under the University's discriminatory admissions program is even more harmful. Blacks and Hispanics admitted to the University as a result of racial discrimination are, on average, far less prepared than their white and Asian classmates.*

DISSENTING OPINION BY JUSTICE GINSBURG

Justice Ginsburg argues that the Texas plan to take students from roughly the top 10 percent of each of the state's public high schools was adopted with the state's racially segregated neighborhoods and schools "front and center stage." So while she applauded the court's decision not to "cast off the equal protection framework" laid out in the Grutter case, "it stops short of reaching the conclusion that framework warrants." She would have, she said, affirmed the judgment of the court of appeals.

Petitioner urges that Texas' Top Ten Percent Law and race-blind holistic review of each application achieve significant diversity, so the University must be content with those alternatives. I have said before and reiterate here that only an ostrich could regard the supposedly neutral alternatives as race unconscious. … I have several times explained why government actors, including state universities, need not be blind to the lingering effects of 'an overtly discriminatory past,' the legacy of 'centuries of law-sanctioned inequality.'

Colleges That Ask Applicants About Brushes With the Law Draw Scrutiny

BY STEPHANIE SAUL | JAN. 28, 2016

THE ONLINE ADMISSIONS application for Auburn University appears simple, until you get to this question on Page 7:

"Have you ever been charged with or convicted of or pled guilty or nolo contendere to a crime other than a minor traffic offense, or are there any criminal charges now pending against you?"

Those who check "yes," even though they have never been convicted of any crime, face extra scrutiny — a call from the admissions office asking for additional information, the university says.

Auburn, in Auburn, Ala., is one of 17 universities in the South that include broad questions on their admissions applications about any contact with the legal system or the police that applicants might have had — even an arrest, with no conviction — according to the Lawyers' Committee for Civil Rights Under Law, an advocacy group. The universities are now the focus of an inquiry by the organization, which says such questions unfairly penalize minorities, who tend to face arrest more frequently and, as a result, could face higher admissions hurdles.

"The disparities and underrepresentation we see at schools is a concern, and this may indeed be one of the contributing factors," said Kristen Clarke, the group's executive director, citing statistics showing low black enrollment at some of the colleges. At Auburn, for example, African-Americans make up 7 percent of the student body in a state where blacks total about 25 percent of the population.

The organization announced Thursday that it would inquire about practices at Auburn and the 16 other institutions that question prospective students about arrests or other contact with the criminal justice system that stops short of a conviction.

The inquiry comes amid growing concern that admissions questions about criminal history and disciplinary action discriminate against black applicants, as a body of statistical evidence emerges showing that black teenagers are singled out for disciplinary action in school and stopped by police at unusually high rates.

The Common Application, used by 600 colleges, does not ask about arrests, but does require applicants to check "yes" or "no" to whether they have been convicted of a crime or faced serious disciplinary action in school.

On Wednesday, New York University's vice president for enrollment management, MJ Knoll-Finn, wrote a letter to both the chairman and the chief executive of the Common Application asking for an expedited review of whether those questions on its form are fair or necessary. N.Y.U. uses the Common Application.

"Especially in the context of high rates of school discipline and incarceration among people of color, it seems vital to pose two questions about the checkboxes: do they, in fact, have any predictive value, and does their presence work against universities' mission as engines of social mobility and diversity either by discouraging applicants or by resulting in unjustified denials of admissions on the grounds of safety or integrity?" Ms. Knoll-Finn's letter said.

A spokeswoman for the Common Application, Aba Blankson, said the group had received N.Y.U.'s letter and was in discussions about the topic, but she declined to discuss details.

A study in 2010 by the Center for Community Alternatives, a nonprofit group in New York, found that 66 percent of colleges ask for criminal history information in admissions, and that some of them look unfavorably even on misdemeanor arrests. At the time, the organization said, the use of such questions appeared to be on the rise after several high-profile criminal cases on university campuses.

Michael Reilly, executive director of the American Association of Collegiate Registrars and Admissions Officers, said that many schools did not like to ask the questions but had been spurred to do so by campus violence. "And they feel they need to do what they can to screen students," he said.

The Lawyers' Committee said it planned to contact the 17 institutions on its list as the first wave of a national initiative aimed at reducing the impact of even minor criminal histories on college admissions. Ms. Clarke said her organization planned to ask the colleges why their application forms included such questions. While the current focus is on universities in seven Southern states, the organization said such questions may be asked by colleges nationwide. The 17 colleges on the group's list include several historically black universities and colleges.

Charles Martin, an Auburn spokesman, said indicating "yes" to the crime question on the application did not disqualify students. "The admissions office calls the applicant directly to obtain more information," he said.

But Ms. Clarke said that in some cases, students might be intimidated and elect not to apply rather than answer the question.

The University of Alabama, where blacks make up 12 percent of the student body, asks prospective students if they are "subject to arrest" and also poses this question: "Have you ever received a written or oral warning not to trespass on public or private property?" A university spokesman, Chris Bryant, said the college had included disciplinary-related questions on its application since 2010, to try to determine whether an applicant's past behavior posed a safety risk. Answering yes to the questions was not an absolute bar to admission, he said, adding that the university was committed to ensuring that its policies were not discriminatory.

The civil-rights group identified Virginia Tech, whose enrollment is 4 percent black, as one of the colleges it would look at. The university's application asks, "Have you ever been arrested or convicted of a violation of any local, state or federal law, other than a minor traffic violation?"

A spokeswoman for Virginia Tech said the university added questions to its application after April 16, 2007, when a student there shot and killed 32 people and wounded 17 others before committing suicide. The student had previously been accused of stalking. "These questions are part of a holistic approach in selecting qualified applicants for undergraduate admission," said the spokeswoman, Tracy Vosburgh. "We do not believe this is racially discriminatory."

In 2014, three New York colleges dropped arrest language from their admissions applications after a request from the state attorney general, Eric T. Schneiderman. "An arrest or police stop that did not result in a conviction, or a criminal record that was sealed or expunged, should not — indeed, must not — be a standard question on a college application," Mr. Schneiderman said at the time.

Supreme Court Upholds Affirmative Action Program at University of Texas

BY ADAM LIPTAK | JUNE 23, 2016

WASHINGTON — The Supreme Court on Thursday rejected a challenge to a race-conscious admissions program at the University of Texas at Austin, handing supporters of affirmative action a major victory.

The decision, Fisher v. University of Texas, No. 14-981, concerned an unusual program and contained a warning to other universities that not all affirmative action programs will pass constitutional muster. But the ruling's basic message was that admissions officials may continue to consider race as one factor among many in ensuring a diverse student body.

The decision, by a 4-to-3 vote, was unexpected. Justice Anthony M. Kennedy, the author of the majority opinion, has long been skeptical of race-sensitive programs and had never before voted to uphold an affirmative action plan. He dissented in the last major affirmative action case.

Supporters of affirmative action hailed the decision as a landmark.

"No decision since Brown v. Board of Education has been as important as Fisher will prove to be in the long history of racial inclusion and educational diversity," said Laurence H. Tribe, a law professor at Harvard, referring to the Supreme Court's 1954 decision striking down segregated public schools.

Roger Clegg, the president of the Center for Equal Opportunity, which supports colorblind policies, said the decision, though disappointing, was only a temporary setback.

"The court's decision leaves plenty of room for future challenges to racial preference policies at other schools," he said. "The struggle goes on."

President Obama hailed the decision. "I'm pleased that the Supreme Court upheld the basic notion that diversity is an important value in our society," he told reporters at the White House. "We are not a country that guarantees equal outcomes, but we do strive to provide an equal shot to everybody."

Justice Kennedy, writing for the majority, said courts must give universities substantial but not total leeway in designing their admissions programs.

"A university is in large part defined by those intangible 'qualities which are incapable of objective measurement but which make for greatness,' " Justice Kennedy wrote, quoting from a landmark desegregation case. "Considerable deference is owed to a university in defining those intangible characteristics, like student body diversity, that are central to its identity and educational mission."

"But still," Justice Kennedy added, "it remains an enduring challenge to our nation's education system to reconcile the pursuit of diversity with the constitutional promise of equal treatment and dignity."

Justices Ruth Bader Ginsburg, Stephen G. Breyer and Sonia Sotomayor joined Justice Kennedy's majority opinion. Justice Elena Kagan, who would probably have voted with the majority, was recused from the case because she had worked on it as solicitor general.

In a lengthy and impassioned dissent delivered from the bench, a sign of deep disagreement, Justice Samuel A. Alito Jr. denounced the court's ruling, saying that the university had not demonstrated the need for race-based admissions and that the Texas program benefited advantaged students over impoverished ones.

"This is affirmative action gone berserk," Justice Alito told his colleagues, adding that what they had done in the case was "simply wrong."

Under the University of Texas' admissions program, most applicants from within the state are admitted under a part of the program that guarantees admission to top students in every high school in the state. This is often called the Top 10 Percent program, though the percentage cutoff can vary by year.

The Top 10 Percent program has produced significant racial and ethnic diversity. In 2011, for instance, 26 percent of freshmen who enrolled under the program were Hispanic, and 6 percent were black. The population of Texas is about 38 percent Hispanic and 12 percent black.

The case challenged a second part of the admissions program. Under it, remaining students from Texas and elsewhere are considered under standards that take into account academic achievement and other factors, including race and ethnicity. Many colleges and universities base all of their admissions decisions on such grounds.

In Grutter v. Bollinger in 2003, the Supreme Court endorsed such free-standing holistic admissions programs, saying it was permissible to consider race as one factor among many to achieve educational diversity. Writing for the majority in that case, Justice Sandra Day O'Connor said she expected that "25 years from now," the "use of racial preferences will no longer be necessary."

Justice Kennedy's decision left Grutter intact.

Thursday's case was brought by Abigail Fisher, a white woman who said the university had denied her admission based on her race. She has since graduated from Louisiana State University.

"I am disappointed that the Supreme Court has ruled that students applying to the University of Texas can be treated differently because of their race or ethnicity," Ms. Fisher said in a statement on Thursday. "I hope that the nation will one day move beyond affirmative action."

When the court last considered Ms. Fisher's case in 2013, supporters of affirmative action were nervous. But the court deferred conclusive action in what appeared to be a compromise decision.

In his dissent on Thursday, Justice Alito said the court had reversed itself. "Something strange has happened since our prior decision in this case," he wrote.

When the second iteration of the case was argued in December, Justice Kennedy suggested that the court might again send it back to the appeals court. On Thursday, though, he said that would have been a waste of time.

"A remand would do nothing more than prolong a suit that has already persisted for eight years and cost the parties on both sides significant resources," he wrote. "Petitioner long since has graduated from another college, and the university's policy — and the data on which it first was based — may have evolved or changed in material ways."

Justice Kennedy then methodically rejected Ms. Fisher's arguments. He said the university's diversity goals were not amorphous but "concrete and precise," satisfying the constitutional requirement that government racial classifications advance a compelling interest.

Justice Alito described those goals — concerning "the destruction of stereotypes," promoting "cross-racial understanding" and preparing students "for an increasingly diverse work force and society" — as slippery and impervious to judicial scrutiny.

Justice Kennedy wrote that the university was justified in saying that the Top Ten Percent plan did not alone produce sufficient diversity, adding that the holistic part of the admissions program "had a meaningful, if still limited, effect on the diversity of the university's freshman class."

He said the Top Ten Percent program had built-in limits.

"An admissions policy that relies exclusively on class rank creates perverse incentives for applicants," he wrote. "Percentage plans 'encourage parents to keep their children in low-performing segregated schools, and discourage students from taking challenging classes that might lower their grade point averages,' " he added, quoting from an earlier dissent from Justice Ginsburg.

"Wherever the balance between percentage plans and holistic review should rest, an effective admissions policy cannot prescribe, realistically, the exclusive use of a percentage plan," Justice Kennedy wrote.

Justice Kennedy's majority opinion was 20 pages long. It elicited a furious 51-page dissent from Justice Alito, joined by Chief Justice John G. Roberts Jr. and Justice Clarence Thomas.

Justice Alito said the majority opinion helped affluent African-American students and hurt Asian-American ones.

"Even though U.T. has never provided any coherent explanation for its asserted need to discriminate on the basis of race, and even though U.T.'s position relies on a series of unsupported and noxious racial assumptions," he wrote, "the majority concludes that U.T. has met its heavy burden. This conclusion is remarkable — and remarkably wrong."

Sherrilyn Ifill, the president of the NAACP Legal Defense and Educational Fund Inc., said the decision was gratifying.

"Universities all over the country are breathing a sigh of relief," she said. "The court very compellingly reaffirmed the importance of diversity."

‘Lopping,’ ‘Tips’ and the ‘Z-List’: Bias Lawsuit Explores Harvard’s Admissions Secrets

BY ANEMONA HARTOCOLLIS, AMY HARMON AND MITCH SMITH | JULY 29, 2018

HE HAD PERFECT SCORES — on his SAT, on three SAT subject tests and on nine Advanced Placement exams — and was ranked first in his high school class of 592. An admissions officer who reviewed his application to Harvard called him “the proverbial picket fence,” the embodiment of the American dream, saying, “Someone we’ll fight over w/ Princeton, I’d guess.”

But in the end, the student was wait-listed and did not get in.

Generations of high school students have applied to Harvard thinking that if they checked all the right boxes, they would be admitted.

But behind the curtain, Harvard’s much-feared admissions officers have a whole other set of boxes that few ambitious high school students and their parents know about — or could check even if they did. The officers speak a secret language — of “dockets,” “the lop list,” “tips,” “DE,” the “Z-list” and the “dean’s interest list” — and maintain a culling system in which factors like where applicants are from, whether their parents went to Harvard, how much money they have and how they fit the school’s goals for diversity may be just as important as scoring a perfect 1600 on the SAT.

This arcane selection process has been illuminated by a lawsuit accusing Harvard of violating federal civil rights law by using racial balancing to shape its admissions in a way that discriminates against Asian-Americans. Harvard says it does not discriminate. Hundreds of admissions documents have been filed in the suit — over the university’s objections that they could reveal trade secrets — and many sections that were previously redacted have been ordered unsealed in recent weeks.

GRETCHEN ERTL FOR THE NEW YORK TIMES

The admissions office at Harvard. A lawsuit against the university has illuminated little-known aspects of its selection process.

To an outsider, the more obscure aspects of Harvard's admissions system might seem transactional and filled with whims and preferences that are raising questions both in court and in public debate. From the university's perspective, those aspects are part of a battle-tested way of building a diverse class of "citizens and citizen-leaders," as Harvard's mission statement puts it, who will help shape the future of society. The system has put brainy future Nobel laureates next to all-star athletes gunning for Wall Street, accomplished musicians and aspiring politicians, the offspring of wealthy alumni and of migrant farmworkers who never got past grade school. It has tapped Jeremy Lin, Malia Obama and Mark Zuckerberg.

"I hope that no student who doesn't get accepted to Harvard — by the way, I wasn't accepted to Harvard College out of high school; I wouldn't let me in, even today — what you hope is that people do not read this as if it's a validation either of who they are nor an invalidation of their potential or their achievement," said Rakesh Khurana, the dean of Harvard College, who went to Cornell as an undergraduate.

"Our goal is not to create a zero-sum game," Professor Khurana added. "We do have some very affirmative goals though that I think are important to understand. That when we talk about diversity of backgrounds and experiences, it includes different academic interests. It includes different occupations of parents. It includes socioeconomic differences. It includes different viewpoints on issues."

SORTING APPLICANTS

The lawsuit, brought by an anti-affirmative-action group called Students for Fair Admissions, has revived the national debate over race-conscious admissions, which is playing out from colleges down to elementary schools.

The case has been orchestrated by Edward Blum, a longtime crusader against affirmative action and voting rights laws, and it may yield him a fresh chance to get the issue before the Supreme Court. The court turned away his last major challenge to university admissions, Fisher v. University of Texas at Austin, in 2016.

The debate goes back to the civil rights movement of the 1950s and '60s. The assassination of the Rev. Dr. Martin Luther King Jr. in 1968 was a turning point, pushing colleges to redouble their efforts to be more representative of American society.

But Asians were an overlooked minority despite a long history of discrimination. As late as 1976, Harvard did not recognize them as a minority group and barred them from a freshman minority orientation banquet. They had a kind of neither-nor identity, denied both the solidarity of other students of color and the social standing of white people.

"There's even a tendency to stay away from each other because you know how, in college, status and prestige are important," said T.K. Chang, who was at Harvard in the mid-70s. Mr. Chang said he found his niche in The Harvard Lampoon, the campus humor magazine.

Since then the stakes in the admissions game have grown. About 40,000 students apply each year, and about 2,000 are admitted for some 1,600 seats in the freshman class. The chances of admission this year were under 5 percent. Of the 26,000 domestic applicants for the Class of 2019 (the lawsuit is not concerned with international students), about 3,500 had perfect SAT math scores, 2,700 had perfect SAT verbal scores, and more than 8,000 had straight A's.

The sorting begins right away. The country is divided into about 20 geographic "dockets," each of which is assigned to a subcommittee of admissions officers with intimate knowledge of that region and its high schools.

Generally two or three admissions officers, or readers, rate applications in five categories: academic, extracurricular, athletic, personal and "overall." They also rate teachers' and guidance counselors' recommendations. And an alumni interviewer also rates the candidates.

Harvard says it also considers "tips," or admissions advantages, for some applicants. The plaintiffs say the college gives tips to five groups: racial and ethnic minorities; legacies, or the children of Harvard or Radcliffe alumni; relatives of a Harvard donor; the children of staff or faculty members; and recruited athletes.

Whether Harvard gives a penalty — in effect, the opposite of a tip — to Asian-Americans goes to the heart of the current litigation. A 1990 report by the Education Department found that, while Harvard was not discriminating against Asian-Americans, it was not giving them a tip, either. A 2013 internal report by Harvard found that being Asian-American was negatively correlated with admission, as did an expert analysis for the plaintiffs. But using a different statistical approach, Harvard's expert found a modest bump for two subgroups of Asian-Americans — women and applicants from California — belying, Harvard said, the overall claim of discrimination.

There are other ways to bolster one's chances of admission, according to the court papers. Savvy alumni hope to gain an advantage for their children by volunteering for Harvard, perhaps by being an admissions interviewer.

It also helps to secure a spot on the "dean's interest list" or the "director's interest list." These are not the familiar lists from academic deans recognizing students with good grades. These lists are named for the dean and director of admissions, and include the names of candidates who are of interest to donors or have connections to Harvard, according to the court papers.

The final decisions are made by a committee of about 40 admissions officers over two or three weeks in March. Meeting in a conference room, they argue over candidates who are "on the bubble" between admission and rejection.

In a deposition running hundreds of pages, William Fitzsimmons — a legendary Harvard hockey goalie, Class of '67, who has been Harvard's admissions dean since 1986 — offered a rare look into the admissions office.

"What is the dean's interest list?" a lawyer for the plaintiffs asked.

"The dean's interest list is something that I would use to make certain that I'm aware of what eventually might happen to that application," Mr. Fitzsimmons replied.

"And how would one go about getting on the dean's interest list?" asked the lawyer, who was prone to calling it the "donor's interest list," in an apparent slip of the tongue.

After an objection from Harvard's lawyer, Mr. Fitzsimmons replied: "In my recruiting process as I go out on the road, I might meet a person at one of the evening meetings, recruiting events, and think just on an impression that this is a person who, you know, might be of interest to the admissions committee. So I might put that person on my interest list."

How about, the plaintiffs' lawyer asked, "if a candidate is of interest to a donor to Harvard, is that something that might land them on the interest list?" Over another objection, Mr. Fitzsimmons replied, "It is possible."

After an exchange running three fully blacked-out pages, Mr. Fitzsimmons explained that candidates on the dean's list could receive a separate rating, in consultation with people connected to the alumni association and the development office, the chief fund-raising arm.

The plaintiffs' lawyer asked, "And are you rating the applicant, or are you rating the level of interest that other people at the university have in this applicant's admission prospect?"

Over an objection, Mr. Fitzsimmons replied, "The latter."

But people on the dean's list often have family who have been involved in the alumni association or scholarship or development work, Mr. Fitzsimmons said, so they know how hard it is to get into Harvard and apply only if they are strong candidates.

The plaintiffs' lawyer asked whether the bigger the financial contribution from a donor, the more it would affect the development office's rating of someone on the dean's list related to that donor. "It would tend to go that way," Mr. Fitzsimmons replied.

Court filings also explore Harvard's little-known Z-list, a sort of back door to admissions.

Harvard is reticent about the Z-list, and much of the information pertaining to it in court papers has been redacted. The list consists of applicants who are borderline academically, the plaintiffs say, but whom Harvard wants to admit. They often have connections. They may be "Z-ed" (yes, a verb) off the wait-list, and are guaranteed admission on the condition that they defer for a year.

About 50 to 60 students a year were admitted through the Z-list for the Classes of 2014 to 2019. They were for the most part white, often legacies or students on the dean's or director's list, the plaintiffs say.

Chuck Hughes, an admissions officer at Harvard from 1995 to 2000, described a special review given to minority applicants while he was there.

Early in his tenure, he said, all competitive applicants had their files studied by at least two readers. He said some minority applicants

GRETCHEN ERTL FOR THE NEW YORK TIMES

Harvard says it tries each year to build a diverse class of "citizens and citizen-leaders" who will help shape the future of society.

would also have their file reviewed by a third reader who was considering the racial composition of the entire class.

"If there was uncertainty on a case in which there were candidates that might have represented minority interests — an Asian-American, an African-American, a Hispanic or a Native American candidate — those would be passed on to someone who was looking at the entire slate of candidates in that particular demographic pool," Mr. Hughes said.

Mr. Hughes said that practice ended early in his time at Harvard.

But the court papers describe a continuing process called "a lop," which the plaintiffs say is used to shape the demographic profile of the class.

As the admissions process winds down, the dean and the director of admissions review the pool of tentatively admitted students and decide how many need to be "lopped," by having their status changed from "admit" to "waitlist" or "deny," the court papers say.

The plaintiffs say that admissions officers then fine-tune the final class using a form that lists five pieces of information about the applicant; they give an example of a form that has spaces for the applicant's name, LIN (lineage), ETH (ethnicity), ATH (athlete), and HFAI (financial aid).

Along the way, Mr. Fitzsimmons, the dean, consults what are called "ethnic stats," which he defines as "any statistics that would give us a sense of where we are in the class regarding ethnicity at that moment." Ethnicity is one of many factors considered in a lop, Mr. Fitzsimmons said in his deposition.

In a response filed in court on Friday, Harvard said that all information in an application file is considered during the lop, and that lopping is not used to control the racial makeup of the class.

The plaintiffs accuse Harvard of jiggering its selection process to create a remarkably stable racial profile from year to year. This year it admitted a class that was almost 23 percent Asian-American; almost 16 percent African-American; and just over 12 percent Latino. The share of admitted students who are Asian-American has risen from 17.6 percent in 2009, and other minorities have gained in concert.

But if Harvard were race-blind, the plaintiffs say, its freshman class would be about 40 percent Asian-American, like the University of California, Berkeley, a public institution that has to abide by a state ban on racial preferences.

As to why the racial and ethnic breakdowns of incoming classes have stayed roughly consistent, Mr. Fitzsimmons said, "from one year to the next, you tend to have roughly the same number and then roughly the same quality from an area."

He added, "It is certainly not a goal of ours to limit ethnicity."

'STRONGER AND BETTER'

The plaintiffs say that the personal rating — which considers an applicant's character and personality — is the most insidious of Harvard's admissions metrics. They say that Asian-Americans are routinely described as industrious and intelligent, but unexceptional and indistinguishable — characterizations that recall painful stereotypes for many people of Asian descent. (The applicant who was the "proverbial picket fence" was Asian-American.)

In the recently unredacted court filings, several Asian-American applicants were described in conspicuously similar terms. One was described as "busy and bright," but the "case will look like many others without late info." Another was "very busy" but "doesn't go extra mile, thus she looks like many w/ this profile." Yet another was "bright & busy" but it was "a bit difficult to see what would hold him in during a lop."

One student was "so very bright but lacking a DE." DE, the court papers say, stands for "distinguishing excellence." Another got a backhanded compliment: "hard worker," but "would she relax and have any fun?"

In Friday's filing, Harvard countered with examples of its positive assessments of applicants of Nepalese, Tibetan, Vietnamese and Indian descent, who were described with words like "deserving," "fascinating" and "Tug for BG," an abbreviation for background. None of the examples the university gave appeared to be of applicants specifically of Chinese or Korean background.

Mr. Hughes, the former Harvard admissions officer, who is now a college admissions consultant, said he warned students of the long odds of getting in for upper- and middle-class applicants, many of whom are white and Asian.

"You don't have first-gen. You don't have son of a police officer. You don't have the immigrant story, or the poor immigrant story, that captivates private colleges and universities," Mr. Hughes said he told his clients. "So those kids just have to be stronger and better."

Other colleges are looking closely at the case. Ted O'Neill, a former dean of admissions at the University of Chicago, said it was easy enough to identify straight-A students who would continue to excel "in the normal terms" throughout their lives.

The hard part, he said, was finding the value in someone that others might not see. "It means passing up," he said. "It means making what looks like unusual choices."

Professor Khurana, the Harvard College dean, acknowledged that Harvard was not always perfect, but said it was trying to get its practices right.

"I have a great deal of humility knowing that some day history will judge us," Professor Khurana said. "I think that's why we are constantly asking ourselves this question: How can we do better? How could we be better? What are we missing? Where are our blind spots?"

JESS BIDGOOD contributed reporting. **ALAIN DELAQUERIERE**, **KATHARINE Q. SEELYE** and **DORIS BURKE** contributed research.

The Rest of the Ivy League Comes to Harvard's Aid in Admissions Challenge

BY ANEMONA HARTOCOLLIS | JULY 30, 2018

THE REST OF THE Ivy League closed ranks behind Harvard on Monday, defending the practice of including the race of applicants in the admissions process in the face of a lawsuit aimed at striking down Harvard's system.

In a joint brief, the seven other members of the Ivy League and nine private universities ranging from M.I.T. to Emory to Stanford said that a ruling against Harvard's admissions process would reverberate across academia and hurt efforts to open higher education to a diverse array of students.

The 16 schools in the amicus brief said they "speak with one voice to emphasize the profound importance of a diverse student body for their educational missions."

But the colleges did not address the specific evidence that those challenging Harvard's system have brought forth. Data that has been released as part of the lawsuit suggests that Asian-American students were held to a higher standard than students of other ethnicities. Harvard denies any discrimination in its admissions process.

The plaintiff, Students for Fair Admissions, an organization representing some Asian-Americans rejected by Harvard, said in its original complaint filed in 2014 that the eight Ivies had remarkably similar proportions of Asian-American students year after year, suggesting that there was some kind of coordinated cap. Harvard has rejected the allegation of any such coordination.

There were a number of briefs supporting Harvard — including from the NAACP Legal Defense and Educational Fund, the American Council on Education and the Lawyers' Committee for Civil Rights Under Law.

GRETCHEN ERTL FOR THE NEW YORK TIMES

The seven other members of the Ivy League said that a ruling against Harvard's admissions process would hurt efforts to open higher education to a diverse array of students.

By Monday afternoon, there was only one brief supporting the plaintiff, from the National Association of Scholars, a group that opposes affirmative action. The group raised Harvard's discrimination against Jews in the 1920s and said Asian-Americans are subjected to similar adverse treatment today. Harvard, in court papers, has argued that the historical record is irrelevant to the current case.

In another amicus brief on behalf of Harvard, Walter Dellinger, a former solicitor general in the Clinton administration, who was succeeded in that post by Seth Waxman, one of Harvard's lawyers in the case, questioned the standing of Students for Fair Admissions to bring the case — even though the judge, Allison D. Burroughs of the Federal District Court in Boston, has already found that the plaintiff does have standing to sue.

Mr. Dellinger, in an apparent reference to Edward Blum, the founder of Students for Fair Admissions, said that case law prohibited "kibitzers, bureaucrats, publicity seekers, and 'cause' mongers from wresting control of litigation from the people directly affected."

Mr. Blum is a staunch opponent of affirmative action who formed Students for Fair Admissions for the express purpose of litigating university admissions cases. Among its members are more than a dozen Asian-American students who were denied admission to Harvard, he said. The group is also suing the University of North Carolina at Chapel Hill.

The NAACP Legal Defense and Educational Fund is representing 21 Harvard student and alumni organizations in its brief. It provided testimonials from people like Catherine Ho, 18, the co-president of the Harvard Asian American Women's Association. Ms. Ho said her parents were refugees from Vietnam who came to the United States because of war. But she said her organization decided to take a position in the lawsuit because it felt solidarity with other "communities of color."

In the declaration she filed with the court, Ms. Ho did, however, express some concern about the allegations of discrimination. "We are frustrated and confused by the data released that suggests problems with how Harvard admissions officers have profiled and described Asian-American applicants," she said.

But she said such problems did not mean that race-conscious admissions should be abandoned altogether. The potential for bias in the personal ratings that some Asian-Americans received in Harvard's admissions review may stem "from ways that principals and teachers describe students," she said in her court declaration.

Justice Dept. Backs Suit Accusing Harvard of Discriminating Against Asian-American Applicants

BY KATIE BENNER | AUG. 30, 2018

WASHINGTON — The Justice Department lent its support on Thursday to students who are suing Harvard University over affirmative action policies that they claim discriminate against Asian-American applicants, in a case that could have far-reaching consequences in college admissions.

In a so-called statement of interest, the department supported the claims of the plaintiffs, a group of Asian-Americans rejected by Harvard. They contend that Harvard has systematically discriminated against them by artificially capping the number of qualified Asian-Americans from attending the school to advance less qualified students of other races.

"Harvard has failed to carry its demanding burden to show that its use of race does not inflict unlawful racial discrimination on Asian-Americans," the Justice Department said in its filing.

The filing said that Harvard "uses a vague 'personal rating' that harms Asian-American applicants' chances for admission and may be infected with racial bias; engages in unlawful racial balancing; and has never seriously considered race-neutral alternatives in its more than 45 years of using race to make admissions decisions."

The Justice Department has increasingly used such statements of interest to intervene in civil rights cases. Before 2006, such statements appeared only seven times in civil rights-oriented disputes, according to a recent paper by law school student Victor Zapana. From 2006 to 2011, they were drafted in at least 242, almost all by the Obama administration on issues such as videotaping police brutality and ensuring that blind people and their service dogs have access to Uber.

But the Trump administration is turning the same tool against affirmative action in college admissions, a major — and highly contentious — legacy of the civil rights era, and one that white conservatives have opposed for decades. In the past few years, the anti-affirmative action cause has been joined by Asian-Americans who argue that they are being held to a higher standard, losing out on coveted slots at places like Harvard as African-Americans, Latinos and other groups get a boost.

A handful of states already ban public universities from relying on affirmative action, pushing several toward a model that takes socioeconomic factors into account instead of race. Public universities in California and Washington have tried to engineer class-based diversity in their student bodies, believing that giving a lift to lower-income students will end up bringing in more minority students as well.

But these methods have not produced classes with an ethnic makeup that mirrors that of the states where they have been used, and many selective private universities continue to admit students partly on the basis of race — though, until Harvard was forced to detail its internal admissions policies recently, few could say how elite universities actually weighed applicants' race.

Now, universities that factor race into admissions have found a powerful new opponent in the Trump administration, which argued in its filing on Thursday that the court should deny Harvard's request to dismiss the case before trial.

The government said that Supreme Court rulings require that universities considering race in admissions meet several standards. They must define their diversity-related goals and show that they cannot meet those goals without using race as a factor in admissions decisions.

The department argued that Harvard does not adequately explain how race factors into its admissions decisions, leaving open the possibility that the university is going beyond what the law allows.

"Harvard has failed to show that it does not unlawfully discriminate against Asian-Americans," the Justice Department said in a statement Thursday.

Harvard said it was "deeply disappointed" but not surprised "given the highly irregular investigation the D.O.J. has engaged in thus far."

"Harvard does not discriminate against applicants from any group, and will continue to vigorously defend the legal right of every college and university to consider race as one factor among many in college admissions, which the Supreme Court has consistently upheld for more than 40 years," the university said in a statement.

A broad coalition of Harvard supporters filed briefs in support of the school Thursday condemning the lawsuit and saying that it would effectively threaten diversity at all American colleges.

Those groups include 25 alumni and student groups represented by the NAACP's Legal Defense and Educational Fund, the American Civil Liberties Union, a group of economists who criticized the experts whose work was used in the original lawsuit and a group of 531 social scientists and academics who study access to college.

"Eliminating race-conscious admissions would disproportionately harm applicants of color, including some Asian-Americans," Harvard alumni said in their filing.

"Applicants' opportunities to amass credentials that make for a competitive college application are greatly affected by race," alumni and students wrote. "Given racial bias in standardized testing and endemic racial inequities," they said the school must continue to consider race.

The Harvard case, which was brought by an anti-affirmative-action group called Students for Fair Admissions, is seen as a test of whether a decades-long effort by conservative politicians and advocates to roll back affirmative action policies will ultimately succeed. The Education and Justice Departments said in July that the administration was abandoning Obama-era policies that asked universities to consider race as a factor in diversifying their campuses and would favor race-blind admissions instead.

Officials from both departments said that the Obama administration had used guidelines to circumvent Congress and the courts to create affirmative action policies that went beyond existing law.

Civil rights leaders and others argue that this stance effectively undermines decades of policy progress that created opportunity for minorities.

The department typically files statements of interest in cases that it believes directly affect the federal government's interests.

"As a recipient of taxpayer dollars, Harvard has a responsibility to conduct its admissions policy without racial discrimination by using meaningful admissions criteria that met lawful requirements," Attorney General Jeff Sessions said in a statement.

In briefs filed in support of Harvard at the end of July, students and alumni said that they "condemn" the plaintiffs' "attempt to manufacture conflict between racial and ethnic groups in order to revive an unrelenting agenda to dismantle efforts to create a racially diverse and inclusive student body through college admissions."

"It's alarming that Trump is aligning himself with anti-civil rights activist Edward Blum in this subversive attempt to say that civil rights protections cause discrimination," said Jeannie Park, the head of the Harvard Asian-American Alumni Alliance and co-founder of the Coalition for a Diverse Harvard, referring to the founder of Students for Fair Admissions. "Trump does not speak for Asian-Americans, just as Blum does not."

At the heart of the case is whether Harvard's admissions staff hold Asian-Americans to higher standards than applicants of other racial or ethnic groups, and whether they use subjective measures, like personal scores, to cap the number of Asian students accepted to the school.

"Harvard today engages in the same kind of discrimination and stereotyping that it used to justify quotas on Jewish applicants in the 1920s and 1930s," Students for Fair Admissions said in a court filing.

Harvard, which admitted less than 5 percent of its applicants this year, said that its own analysis did not find discrimination.

A trial in the case has been scheduled for October.

If it winds its way to the Supreme Court, it could be heard by Judge Brett M. Kavanaugh, Mr. Trump's nominee for the vacant seat once held by Justice Anthony M. Kennedy. The case could have far-reaching implications for the nation's colleges and universities that consider race in their admissions processes. The Justice Department is pursuing its own investigation into Harvard's admissions policies based on a complaint it received.

The Obama administration used statements of interest in novel ways to further its civil rights agenda, sometimes by making the unusual move of intervening in local cases.

In 2013, the Justice Department intervened in a local case in Burlington, Wash., where poor people contended that their public lawyers were too overworked to adequately do their jobs. The Obama administration also intervened in local legal disputes over legal aid issues in New York, juvenile prisoners in California and transgender students in Michigan.

The Trump administration has filed statements of interest on other charged topics this year. In February it supported the plaintiffs who are suing pharmaceutical companies and drug distributors in a sprawling, prescription opioids lawsuit in Ohio. This month it supported the merits of a suit that says Facebook abets discriminatory housing practices.

VIVIAN YEE contributed reporting from New York.

What's at Stake in the Harvard Lawsuit? Decades of Debate Over Race in Admissions

BY ANEMONA HARTOCOLLIS | OCT. 13, 2018

AT A TIME OF deepening racial and political divisions among Americans, a trial widely perceived to be a referendum on affirmative action will begin on Monday in Boston, bringing into a courtroom decades of fierce disputes over whether Harvard University and other elite institutions use racial balancing to shape their classes.

The case accuses Harvard of setting a quota on Asian-American students accepted to the university and holding them to a higher standard than applicants of other races. It flips the strategy used in past challenges to race-conscious admissions: Instead of arguing that the school disadvantages whites, the plaintiffs say that Harvard is admitting minority groups and white students over another minority, Asian-Americans.

Asian-Americans are divided on the case, with some saying they are being unfairly used as a wedge in a brazen attempt to abolish affirmative action. But it is not yet clear whether the case will make new law — perhaps banning the consideration of race in college admissions — or will narrowly affect only Harvard. Legal experts say at the very least, the case will expose the sometimes arcane admissions practices of one of the most selective institutions in the world.

At most, it could make its way to a newly more conservative Supreme Court and change the face of college admissions.

"I definitely think that this will affect the fate of affirmative action and therefore racial diversity in universities across the country," said Nicole Gon Ochi, a lawyer for Asian Americans Advancing Justice in Los Angeles. "It's about much more than a few elite universities like Harvard."

The case is particularly resonant, experts say, because Harvard's "holistic" admissions policy, which considers race as one factor among many, has been held up as a model by the Supreme Court since a landmark affirmative action case in 1978, and is effectively the law of the land. Harvard says that it does not discriminate, but considers each student individually to build a class of diverse backgrounds, races, talents and ideas.

The trial will unfold as millions of high school students are figuring out how to define themselves in their college applications. It comes as heated political campaigns fought over racial and economic fault lines culminate in midterm elections.

And it comes as the Trump administration continues to tip its hand toward the plaintiffs. The Justice Department has filed a statement of interest in the case. It has opened its own inquiries into complaints of discrimination against Asian-Americans, at Harvard and at Yale. And in July, the Education and Justice Departments withdrew Obama-era guidelines that encouraged the consideration of race in college admissions.

The rest of the Ivy League has closed ranks behind Harvard, filing a joint amicus brief, and universities across the nation are watching intently for a ruling with wide-ranging impacts.

The lawsuit says that Harvard holds the proportions of each race in its classes roughly constant and manipulates a vague "personal" admissions rating to downgrade applications from Asian-Americans. By doing this, the suit says, Harvard is violating federal civil rights law, which prohibits discrimination by universities that receive federal funds.

Harvard says there is no evidence that the 40-member admissions committee has engaged in any orchestrated scheme to limit the admission of Asian-Americans. But it says that eliminating the consideration of race would cut the number of African-American, Hispanic and other underrepresented minorities by nearly half.

The lawsuit was filed in 2014 but has been generations in the making.

Suspicions that Harvard and other top colleges were imposing informal quotas on Asian-Americans to combat their quickly growing presence among the academic elite date back to at least the 1980s. In 1988, the Office for Civil Rights of the federal Education Department opened an investigation but cleared Harvard of racial discrimination.

Many remained wary. The Education Department looked into a new admissions complaint about Asian-Americans in 2012, ultimately deciding not to investigate, according to court documents. The same year, Ron Unz, a conservative activist and Harvard graduate, published a lengthy dissection of Harvard admissions, suggesting that the university was keeping down the number of Asian-American students. The essay helped rekindle public debate on the issue.

Harvard appears to have taken the criticism seriously. Around that time, an internal research group at the university conducted a study of admissions, asking, "Does the admissions process disadvantage Asians?" It found that being Asian-American decreased the chances of admission.

Much of the plaintiffs' case echoes the findings.

Harvard says the internal study was preliminary and incomplete, and that the plaintiffs have cherry-picked data, used innuendo and taken documents out of context to arrive at their conclusions.

Past Supreme Court decisions on affirmative action limited the use of race in college admissions without banning it outright. The court has said that an applicant's race can be used as a "plus factor" or "a factor of a factor of a factor," terms that are purposefully ambiguous.

"The Supreme Court has been vague about what is O.K.," William Baude, a law professor at the University of Chicago, said. "It seems like they say it's O.K. as long as it's not too much or too blatant. And then the other problem is that the schools have been very secretive about exactly what they do. Which means we don't know what the law exactly is, and we don't know whether anybody is obeying."

Legal experts say the Harvard case could be a fact-based trial, specific to one university. But if it is appealed, the Supreme Court could have a chance to revisit the law on affirmative action. That is the game plan of the plaintiffs, Students for Fair Admissions, a group formed by a conservative activist against affirmative action, Edward Blum. Mr. Blum has recruited for the group nearly two-dozen Asian-American students who were rejected by Harvard.

"It's important to recognize that the fate of affirmative action doctrine and Harvard don't necessarily go in the same direction," Professor Baude said. "Affirmative action could stay the same even if Harvard loses. The challengers have both goals. They both think that what's happening at Harvard is wrong, and they think the whole regime is wrong, and they'd like to use this case to prove it."

S.F.F.A. has other irons in the fire. It has also filed a complaint challenging race-conscious admissions, but not focusing on Asian-Americans, at the University of North Carolina at Chapel Hill. It is scheduled for trial in the spring, and is also intended to land in higher courts.

Mr. Blum was the architect of Fisher v. University of Texas at Austin, the last major affirmative action case to go to the Supreme Court, which he lost in 2016. But Justice Samuel A. Alito Jr.'s dissent in the case, in which a white woman said she was denied admission because of her race, hinted that discrimination against Asian-American students could be fertile ground for litigation.

Ilya Shapiro, a senior fellow at the libertarian Cato Institute, said affirmative action could be vulnerable if the lawsuit goes to the Supreme Court and the newly appointed Justice Brett M. Kavanaugh follows the lead of the chief justice, John G. Roberts Jr.

"On this issue, John Roberts has written that the only way to stop discriminating on race is to stop discriminating on race," Mr. Shapiro said. "So he has made up his mind that racial preferences are improper in any way."

Harvard's newly installed president, Lawrence Bacow, issued an email this past week saying he was confident the university would prevail, and pleaded for civility and the long view.

“Reasonable people may have different views,” Mr. Bacow said. “I would hope all of us recognize, however, that we are members of one community — and will continue to be so long after this trial is in the rearview mirror.”

DORIS BURKE, **SUSAN BEACHY** and **KITTY BENNETT** contributed research.

I'm for Affirmative Action. Can You Change My Mind?

OPINION | BY GARY GUTTING | DEC. 10, 2018

I have a rational argument for my position. But I want to hear yours.

AFFIRMATIVE ACTION FOR minorities in college admissions is once again under serious challenge. For many opponents, the heart of the case against is made by Chief Justice John Roberts's pithy comment "The way to stop discrimination on the basis of race is to stop discriminating on the basis of race." The dictum seems to be trivially true — a repetition of the same claim in almost the same words, what logicians call a tautology, like a dog is a dog.

Of course, the claim is not quite that simple. In context, it's clear that Chief Justice Roberts means "The way to stop discrimination against any given race is to stop discriminating against all races." This is not a tautology, but it does seem plausible: If you think it's wrong to discriminate against minority applicants, shouldn't you also think it's wrong to discriminate against majority (white) applicants? If so, you shouldn't support affirmative action, since it allows admitting minorities rather than whites precisely because of their race.

I don't want to deny the strength of this argument. It seems implicit in, for example, the 1964 Civil Rights Act, which says it is illegal "to discriminate against any individual ... because of such individual's race, color, religion, sex, or national origin." And over the past 50 years, the idea that race should not matter in judgments of merit has become widely accepted among Americans. Affirmative action, however, denies this: When the purpose is sufficiently worthy, it's right to prefer minority over majority applicants (and even to prefer some minorities over other minorities, such as Asian-Americans).

So the question becomes, what purpose justifies preferring minority applicants? What problem do we need affirmative action to solve? The straightforward answer is the underrepresentation of minorities in elite colleges and universities, where the percentage of minorities is far below their percentage of the population. So, for example, blacks make up 15 percent of the college-age population but only 6 percent of those enrolled at the top 100 private and public schools. There's little hope of improvement without further action, since the figures have scarcely changed since 1980. (At universities below the top 100, minorities are not underrepresented.)

The underrepresentation does not seem due to admissions committees' prejudices, conscious or unconscious, that blind them to the objective credentials of minority applicants. Those rejected have lower test scores and less impressive academic and extracurricular achievements. Some argue that these standard criteria are themselves unfair and that other factors, such as strength of character, are at least as important. Writing at The Washington Post, the Stanford education professor Linda Darling-Hammond and the venture capitalist Ted Dintersmith suggest that it may be "more about grit than GPAs." But judgment about moral and emotional qualities can be highly subjective, and there's no reason to think that over all, minority students are superior in these qualities.

Making the case for affirmative action requires admitting that the minority students chosen will not fully meet the standard criteria of admission. How can this be anything other than unjust discrimination? Supreme Court Justice Sonia Sotomayor suggests an answer in her response to Chief Justice Roberts's famous comment: "The way to stop discrimination on the basis of race is to speak openly and candidly on the subject of race, and to apply the Constitution with eyes open to the unfortunate effects of centuries of racial discrimination."

The last step, then, in the defense of affirmation action in college admissions is an appeal to the moral demand to compensate for the damage done to minorities by a long history of racial discrimination. Sotomayor elaborates: "Race matters in part because of the long history of racial minorities being denied access to the political process. ... Race also matters because of persistent racial inequality in society — inequality that cannot be ignored and that has produced stark socioeconomic disparities. ... Race matters because of the slights, the snickers, the silent judgments that reinforce that most crippling of thoughts: 'I do not belong here.' "

What exactly is the logic here? We know the horrors of slavery, Jim Crow and lynchings, but how could they connect to the somewhat less than stellar academic records of middle-class black students who might not make the cut at Harvard? The connection would have to lie, as Sotomayor suggests, in the present-day residues, the stubborn structural effects of centuries of mistreatment, gradually diminishing but still an undeserved burden.

The burden shows up in both economic and social terms. The wealth (total value of home, savings, investments, etc.) of middle-class white families is about four times that of middle-class black families. This gives white families a decided edge in their ability to survive financial setbacks and resources to provide a better education for their children. Similarly, due to restrictive real estate practices, wealthier blacks still often live in poorer neighborhoods than comparable whites do, reducing educational and cultural opportunities. There are also psychological effects: Black children live in a world where their very appearance presents them as "others," often objects of either uneasy suspicion or patronizing sympathy.

So it's hard to deny that blacks as a whole face a distinctive set of disadvantages that are primarily due to the still effective legacy of slavery. But why think affirmative action will be an appropriate remedy? Chief Justice Roberts and others suggest that simply knowing that they are at an elite school in large part because of their race will increase minority students' alienation and self-doubt. To this, one common response is that athletes and legacy admissions don't seem bothered by such concerns. But they at least can see their admission as due to their own or their families' distinctive achievements. On the other hand, why shouldn't black students be proud to see themselves as very talented people who are a vanguard in one small effort to undo the evils of their history? And shouldn't they expect that their children and grandchildren will move further and further toward a world where that history will eventually become truly past?

I think I've made a strong case for affirmative action, although I can see how some readers might reasonably oppose it. To those who do, I would ask that you reflect on the way affirmative action could be a viable step toward closing our painful racial divide.

GARY GUTTING is an emeritus professor of philosophy at Notre Dame and the author, most recently, of "Talking God: Philosophers on Belief," a collection of interviews with philosophers on religion.

CHAPTER 5

The Future of Affirmative Action

Today, the political and discriminatory landscape is shifting. The Trump administration has stated that it aims to reverse Obama-era affirmative action policies, but the implications of this are unclear. Maybe the direction affirmative action was heading created opportunities for universities to be more selective. The use of racial quotas, for example, seems to have come to a tipping point, now hindering minorities instead of assuring a non-discriminating meritocracy. Meanwhile, issues such as the gender gap in employment and pay equality are looking for support. Does affirmative action have a place in the evolving landscape or has it become too antiquated for modern challenges?

If Affirmative Action Is Doomed, What's Next?

BY DAVID LEONHARDT | JUNE 17, 2014

AFFIRMATIVE ACTION AS we know it is probably doomed.

When you ask top Obama administration officials and people in the federal court system about the issue, you often hear a version of that prediction.

Five of the Supreme Court's nine justices have never voted in favor of a race-based affirmative action program. Already, the court has ruled that such programs have the burden of first showing "that available, workable race-neutral alternatives do not suffice."

Two Alternatives to Today's Affirmative Action

If affirmative action revolved around income rather than race, classes would be roughly as racially diverse as they are now, but more diverse economically. Alternately, basing admissions decisions on high-school rank would increase both forms of diversity.

Diversity of student body, measured two ways, at 193 of America's most selective colleges, under three different admissions approaches.

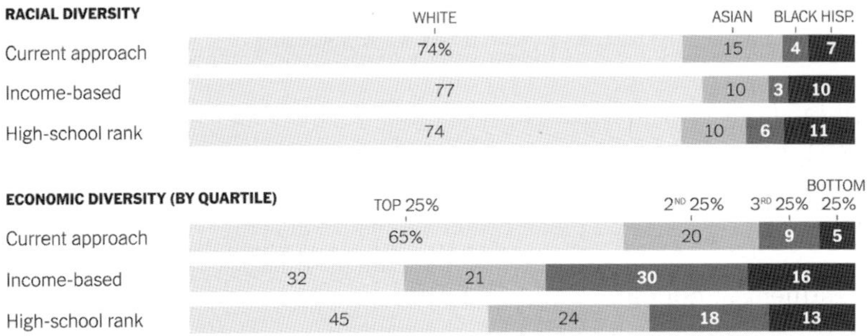

THE NEW YORK TIMES

The income-based approach includes parents' income, education and occupation, characteristics of the student's high school and other factors. High-school rank is based on test scores. For example, the student with the highest SAT score at a given school would be ranked first at that school.

The issue appears to be following a familiar path in Chief Justice John Roberts's court. On divisive social issues, the Roberts court first tends to issue narrow rulings, with the backing of both conservative and liberal justices, as my colleague Adam Liptak has noted. In later terms, the five conservative justices deliver a more sweeping decision, citing the earlier case as precedent. With affirmative action, last year's case involving Texas could be the first stage.

Beyond the Supreme Court, eight states have already banned race-based affirmative action, and four additional ones, including Ohio and Missouri, may consider bans soon.

Despite this reality, many supporters of affirmative action are in some version of denial. Top university officials say that the court hasn't prohibited their approach yet and say they hope it never will. Few colleges or companies are trying innovative approaches.

Two new books aim to fill the void. They lay out detailed visions of an affirmative action that would combine racial and economic diversity — in contrast to the current version, which has done little to promote economic diversity. Above all, the books answer the common liberal concern that economic-based affirmative action is a bad substitute for race-based affirmative action.

"Race-based affirmative action is a blunt instrument that doesn't help the vast majority of black and Latino kids," says Sheryll Cashin, who is the author of one of the new books, "Place, Not Race" (Beacon Press), as well as a Georgetown University law professor and a former clerk to Justice Thurgood Marshall. "And ironically it engenders resentments that make it harder to build multiracial alliances to build investment in education."

The insight of both books is that the obstacles facing many black and Latino children can be captured through a set of variables that are, on the surface, race-neutral. A system based on these factors, rather than race per se, would be undeniably constitutional and more politically popular.

The most obvious of the factors is income — but it is not the most important. Supporters of today's affirmative action often point out that a strictly income-based version of the program would produce much less racial diversity, and they're right. Fewer than one-third of households making $40,000 a year or less are black or Latino, according to census data.

But income alone understates the challenges facing many minority children. Black and Latino students are more likely to live in poor neighborhoods than white and Asian students with similar incomes. Black and Latino families are also less wealthy than white and Asian families. And black children in particular are much more likely to be growing up without two parents in their home.

Proponents of a new kind of affirmative action prefer an approach that focuses on wealth, neighborhood and family structure, as well as parents' income, education and other factors. Doing so steers clear of the legal restrictions on racial classifications — and, in the minds of most Americans, is fair. Is an affluent teenager with a 1,300 SAT score

EVELYN HOCKSTEIN FOR THE NEW YORK TIMES

Anthony P. Carnevale, one of the authors of "The Future of Affirmative Action."

really more accomplished than the valedictorian of a troubled high school with a 1,250? No.

The second new book — "The Future of Affirmative Action," which comes out Tuesday — includes a detailed analysis of class-based systems, from Anthony Carnevale, Stephen Rose and Jeff Strohl. The bottom line is that they would vastly increase economic diversity while leaving broadly similar racial diversity. Under some systems, particularly those that emphasize students' high-school rank, racial diversity would increase. Using high-school rank — as Texas has done — is so powerful because of today's high levels of economic and racial segregation.

"Universities have long said, 'We can get racial diversity only if we use race,'" said Richard Kahlenberg, the editor of the book, which The Century Foundation and Lumina Foundation are publishing. "There are a number of ways to produce racial diversity without using race."

Of course, they would cost universities more than the current system. Today, students at top colleges (and, by extension, at elite

EVELYN HOCKSTEIN FOR THE NEW YORK TIMES

Sheryll Cashin, the author of "Place, Not Race."

employers) come from different races, religions, regions and even countries — but are overwhelmingly well-off. On the other hand, the colleges that are most aggressive about affirmative action are also the ones with the most money.

The biggest downside to these class-based approaches is that they don't acknowledge the role that race plays in American society. If you somehow found otherwise identical white and black students — living in the same neighborhood, with the same income, wealth and structure — the black student would still probably have to do more just to keep up. Racism is not dead, as social-science research makes clear.

In the workplace, résumés with typically black names are less likely to receive callbacks than identical résumés with typically white names, one study found. Another found that, on eBay, iPods pictured being held by a dark-skinned hand sold for less than those being held by light-skinned hands. (The name of the paper is "The Visible Hand.")

But here's the paradox for defenders of today's affirmative action: Their best hope of salvaging some form of it is to make race secondary and class primary.

Justice Anthony Kennedy, the swing vote on the Supreme Court, has signaled some openness to letting institutions consider race, so long as race doesn't dominate their decisions. And in today's version of affirmative action, race dominates. The standard way that colleges judge any potential alternative is to ask whether it results in precisely the same amount of racial diversity, rather than acknowledging that other forms of diversity also matter.

An affirmative action based mostly on class, and using race in narrowly tailored ways, is one much more likely to win approval from Justice Kennedy when the issue inevitably returns to the court.

The next move belongs to those who believe in affirmative action. They can continue to hope against hope that the status quo will somehow hold. Or they can begin to experiment — and maybe end up with a fairer system than the current one.

Making Affirmative Action White Again

OPINION | BY IRA KATZNELSON | AUG. 12, 2017

JEFF SESSIONS TOLD the Senate Judiciary Committee 20 years ago that affirmative action irritated people (he meant white people) because it could cause them to lose opportunities "simply because of their race." This sense of grievance lies behind the Justice Department's recent memo seeking lawyers to investigate "race-based discrimination" in college admissions.

It also implies that all that stands between hard-working whites and success are undeserving minorities who are doled out benefits, including seats at good schools, by reckless government agents.

In fact, today's socioeconomic order has been significantly shaped by federally backed affirmative action for whites. The most important pieces of American social policy — the minimum wage, union rights, Social Security and even the G.I. Bill — created during and just after the Great Depression, conferred enormous benefits on whites while excluding most Southern blacks.

Southern Democrats in Congress did this by carving out occupational exclusions; empowering local officials who were hostile to black advancement to administer the policies; and preventing antidiscrimination language from appearing in social welfare programs.

New Deal and Fair Deal initiatives created a modern middle class by enabling more Americans to attend college, secure good jobs, buy houses and start businesses. But in the waning days of Jim Crow, as a result of public policy, many African-Americans were blocked from these opportunities and fell even further behind their white counterparts. The country missed the chance to build an inclusive middle class.

The congressmen from the 17 states that practiced legal segregation constituted a pivotal bloc. When Southern-led congressional committees drafted the law that created the Social Security program in 1935, they excluded maids and farmworkers, the two dominant job categories for Southern blacks and Southwestern Latinos, from the program. This denied benefits to 66 percent of African-Americans across the country, and as much as 80 percent of Southern blacks. It also disproportionately hurt Mexican-Americans.

These exclusions "reinforced the semblance of a caste system of labor in the South and Southwest," according to a recent study by the scholar David Stoesz. "Absent a government safety net, minority workers had to work at any wage available, until they dropped." Although the exclusions were eliminated in the 1950s, it proved difficult for these workers to catch up, since the program required at least five years of contributions before benefits could be received.

Southern legislators introduced the same job category exclusions into other New Deal laws: the Wagner Act of 1935 that helped to expand industrial unions, the Fair Labor Standards Act of 1938 that mandated a 40-hour workweek and a minimum wage that explicitly left out agricultural and domestic workers.

Representative James Wilcox, a Depression-era Florida Democrat, explained the region's position during the Fair Labor Standards Act debate: "You cannot put the Negro and the white man on the same basis and get away with it," he declared.

When Congress passed the G.I. Bill in 1944 to help white veterans buy homes, attend college, get job training and start business ventures, it could have done the same for blacks. But at Southern lawmakers' insistence, local officials administered these benefits. As a result, Southern blacks were left out, except for low-level vocational training. The law accommodated segregation in higher education, created job ceilings imposed by local officials, and tolerated local banks' unwillingness to approve federally insured mortgages or small-business loans for African-Americans and Latinos.

When the federal government aided home buyers with the National Housing Act of 1934, which insured private mortgages, it might also have warded off housing segregation and helped blacks purchase homes. Instead, it supported racist covenants and typically denied mortgages to blacks. This legacy persists. The median household wealth for white families, which consists primarily of equity in housing, stands today at $134,230, according to the Economic Policy Institute. But for African-American families, it is just $11,030.

The unsettling history of this affirmative action for whites significantly widened racial gaps in income, wealth and opportunity that continue to scar American life.

The anti-affirmative-action radicalism of the Justice Department's memo is wrapped in misleading language of fair play. If pursued, it would once again deploy the power of government and the majesty of law to fortify rather than diminish the effects of the country's long history of racial oppression.

The Justice Department's document is more than historically ignorant. It mocks the mission and history of its own Civil Rights Division, which Attorney General William P. Rogers, a Republican, created in 1957 to fight Jim Crow restrictions on black voting.

Since then, the division has fought school segregation, enforced fair housing law and defended voting rights. So it is surreal to imagine that its authority might be deployed to weaken or eliminate policies in higher education that increase racial diversity.

Even the George W. Bush administration sought to underscore its civil rights commitments. A Bush assistant attorney general, Wan J. Kim, extolled the division's election monitoring and Voting Rights Act enforcement lawsuits, as well as its court cases on fair lending and fair housing.

Though President Bush spoke out in 2003 to support lawsuits against affirmative action at the University of Michigan, both he and the Justice Department's amicus brief supported the diversity rationale that the Supreme Court eventually upheld in Grutter v. Bollinger and backed last year in Fisher v. University of Texas.

"America is a diverse country, racially, economically and ethnically," Mr. Bush said in 2003. "And our institutions of higher education should reflect our diversity."

What the Trump administration is considering would go well beyond attempts by the Bush White House to curtail some aspects of affirmative action. By pushing back against efforts to rectify generations of racial discrimination and exclusion in colleges, the current Justice Department seems unwilling to remain within the framework that Justice Lewis Powell articulated in 1978 in University of California v. Bakke, which was later affirmed in the Grutter and Fisher decisions. This view recognizes diversity as an appropriate and legitimate rationale for admissions policies.

Any decision to reorient the Civil Rights Division would be based on the fiction that we already possess a level playing field. Perhaps more disturbing is how such a Sessions-Trump policy would further encourage white resentment. Polls show that a near majority of Trump voters believe that actions to achieve diversity have come at the expense of whites.

Over the decades, the excluded and their allies have understood the stakes when they pushed for effective affirmative action and fought to make the social safety net available to all Americans. Properly heeded, their rallying cries would help the country's working people across racial lines a great deal more than the race-baiting projects the Trump administration is pursuing.

IRA KATZNELSON is a professor of political science and history at Columbia University, president of the Social Science Research Council and the author of "When Affirmative Action Was White."

Trump Officials Reverse Obama's Policy on Affirmative Action in Schools

BY ERICA L. GREEN, MATT APUZZO AND KATIE BENNER | JULY 3, 2018

WASHINGTON — The Trump administration said Tuesday that it was abandoning Obama administration policies that called on universities to consider race as a factor in diversifying their campuses, signaling that the administration will champion race-blind admissions standards.

In a joint letter, the Education and Justice Departments announced that they had rescinded seven Obama-era policy guidelines on affirmative action, which, the departments said, "advocate policy preferences and positions beyond the requirements of the Constitution."

"The executive branch cannot circumvent Congress or the courts by creating guidance that goes beyond the law and — in some instances — stays on the books for decades," said Devin M. O'Malley, a Justice Department spokesman.

Striking a softer tone, Education Secretary Betsy DeVos wrote in a separate statement: "The Supreme Court has determined what affirmative action policies are constitutional, and the court's written decisions are the best guide for navigating this complex issue. Schools should continue to offer equal opportunities for all students while abiding by the law."

The Trump administration's moves come with affirmative action at a crossroads. Hard-liners in the Justice and Education Departments are moving against any use of race as a measurement of diversity in education. And the retirement of Justice Anthony M. Kennedy at the end of this month will leave the Supreme Court without its swing vote on affirmative action while allowing President Trump to nominate a justice opposed to policies that for decades have tried to integrate elite educational institutions.

A highly anticipated case is pitting Harvard against Asian-American students who say one of the nation's most prestigious institutions has systematically excluded some Asian-American applicants to maintain slots for students of other races. That case is clearly aimed at the Supreme Court.

"The whole issue of using race in education is being looked at with a new eye in light of the fact that it's not just white students being discriminated against, but Asians and others as well," said Roger Clegg, the president and general counsel of the conservative Center for Equal Opportunity. "As the demographics of the country change, it becomes more and more problematic."

Democrats and civil rights organizations denounced the administration's decisions. Representative Nancy Pelosi of California, the House Democratic leader, said the "rollback of vital affirmative action guidance offends our nation's values" and called it "yet another clear Trump administration attack on communities of color."

Guidance documents like those rescinded on Tuesday do not have the force of law, but they amount to the official view of the federal government. School officials who keep their race-conscious admissions policies intact would do so knowing that they could face a Justice Department investigation or lawsuit, or lose funding from the Education Department.

The Obama administration believed that students benefited from being surrounded by diverse classmates, so in 2011, the administration offered schools a potential road map to establishing affirmative action policies and race-based considerations that could withstand legal scrutiny from an increasingly skeptical Supreme Court.

In a pair of policy guidance documents issued in 2011, the Obama Education and Justice Departments informed elementary and secondary schools and college campuses of "the compelling interests" established by the Supreme Court to achieve diversity. They concluded that the court "has made clear such steps can include taking account of the race of individual students in a narrowly tailored manner."

But Trump Justice Department officials identified those documents as particularly problematic and full of "hypotheticals" intended to allow schools to skirt the law.

The Trump administration's decision returned the government's policies to the George W. Bush era. The administration did not formally reissue the Bush-era guidance but in recent days did repost a Bush administration affirmative action policy document online. That document states, "The Department of Education strongly encourages the use of race-neutral methods for assigning students to elementary and secondary schools." For several years, that document had been replaced by a note declaring that the policy had been withdrawn.

The Education Department had last reaffirmed its position on affirmative action in schools in 2016 after a Supreme Court ruling said schools could consider race as one factor among many. In that case, Fisher v. University of Texas at Austin, a white woman claimed she was denied admission because of her race.

"It remains an enduring challenge to our nation's education system to reconcile the pursuit of diversity with the constitutional promise of equal treatment and dignity," Justice Kennedy wrote for the 4-to-3 majority.

Some colleges, such as Duke and Bucknell universities, said they would wait to see how the Education Department proceeds in issuing new guidance. Other colleges said they would proceed with diversifying their campuses as the Supreme Court intended.

Melodie Jackson, a Harvard spokeswoman, said the university would "continue to vigorously defend its right, and that of all colleges and universities, to consider race as one factor among many in college admissions, which has been upheld by the Supreme Court for more than 40 years."

A spokeswoman for the University of Michigan, which won a major Supreme Court case in 2003, suggested that the flagship university would like more freedom to consider race, not less. But it is already constrained by state law. After the case, Michigan voters enacted a constitutional ban on race-conscious college admissions policies.

"We believe the U.S. Supreme Court got it right in 2003 when it affirmed our law school's approach at the time, which allowed consideration of race as one of many factors in the admissions process," said Kim Broekhuizen, the Michigan spokeswoman. "We still believe that."

Attorney General Jeff Sessions has indicated that he will take a tough line against such views. Federal prosecutors will investigate and sue universities over discriminatory admissions policies, he said.

But a senior Justice Department official denied that these decisions were rolling back protections for minorities. He said they were instead hewing the department closer to the letter of the law. In the departments' letter, officials wrote that "the protections from discrimination on the basis of race remain in place."

"The departments are firmly committed to vigorously enforcing these protections on behalf of all students," the letter said.

Anurima Bhargava, who headed civil rights enforcement in schools for the Justice Department under President Barack Obama and helped write that administration's guidance, said the withdrawal of the guidelines was timed for brief filings in the Harvard litigation, due at the end of the month.

"This is a wholly political attack," Ms. Bhargava said. "And our schools are the place where our communities come together, so our schools have to continue to promote diversity and address segregation, as the U.S. Constitution demands."

Catherine Lhamon, who served as the Education Department's head of civil rights under Mr. Obama, called the departments' move confusing.

"There's no reason to rethink or reconsider this, as the Supreme Court is the highest court in the land and has spoken on this issue," Ms. Lhamon said.

On Friday, the Education Department began laying the groundwork for the shift, when it restored on its civil rights website the Bush-era guidance. Conservative advocacy groups saw that as promising. Mr. Clegg, of the Center for Equal Opportunity, said that preserving the Obama-era guidance would be akin to "the F.B.I. issuing a document on how you can engage in racial profiling in a way where you won't get caught."

Ms. DeVos has seemed hesitant to wade in on the fate of affirmative action policies, which date back to a 57-year-old executive order by President John F. Kennedy, who recognized systemic and discriminatory disadvantages for women and minorities. The Education Department did not partake in the Justice Department's formal interest in Harvard's litigation.

"I think this has been a question before the courts and the courts have opined," Ms. DeVos told The Associated Press.

But Ms. DeVos's new head of civil rights, Kenneth L. Marcus, may disagree. A vocal opponent of affirmative action, Mr. Marcus was confirmed last month on a party-line Senate vote, and it was Mr. Marcus who signed Tuesday's letter.

Under Mr. Marcus's leadership, the Louis D. Brandeis Center, a human rights organization that champions Jewish causes, filed an amicus brief in 2012, the first time the Supreme Court heard Fisher v. University of Texas at Austin. In the brief, the organization argued that "race conscious admission standards are unfair to individuals, and unhealthy for society at large."

The organization argued that Asian-American students were particularly victimized by race "quotas" that were once used to exclude Jewish people.

As the implications for affirmative action for college admissions play out in court, it is unclear what the decision holds for elementary and secondary schools. New York City is embroiled in a debate about whether to change its entrance standard — currently a single test — for its most prestigious high schools to allow for more black and Latino students.

ANEMONA HARTOCOLLIS contributed reporting from New York.

The Curse of Affirmative Action

OPINION | BY BRET STEPHENS | OCT. 19, 2018

A lawsuit challenges Harvard's betrayal of "Veritas."

OF ALL THE NAMES I've been called in life, including the usual anti-Semitic slurs, none has more sting than "affirmative action hire."

I got that a lot on social media after I joined The Times. The meaning was clear: I was a quota-filler who had taken the place of somebody more deserving. Whatever I had accomplished, through talent or hard work, wasn't enough. I was just fulfilling a misbegotten mandate for ideological diversity — and doing even that poorly, since, like every other columnist here, I'm also a Trump opponent.

The accusation always came from the left, and it contained an implicit admission. The very people who ordinarily championed affirmative action as a cornerstone of a decent society — for giving a needed leg up to the systemically disadvantaged — had no trouble understanding the other dimension of the policy — an unfair preference for the unqualified. They knew that "affirmative action," whatever its benefits as a form of social engineering, was a synonym for mediocrity.

They also knew the insult's insidious psychological power to wound. To be told that you are an affirmative action hire shakes the ground under your feet. Am I being *humored*? Have I always been? Is coming to The Times a mark of professional merit, or is my job a polite fiction, one that everyone but me sees through?

I mention this as the most significant legal battle over affirmative action in recent years unfolds in a Boston courtroom. In *Students for Fair Admissions v. Harvard*, a federal judge is considering whether Harvard University has violated the civil rights of Asian-Americans by using vague measures of personality to hold down their chances of admission.

Evidence: An internal Harvard document from 2013 found that, based on admissions criteria that considered academic performance only, Asian-Americans would account for 43 percent of the admitted class. But their actual admission rate was 19 percent then and has risen to only 23 percent since.

Evidence: An analysis commissioned by the plaintiffs of student records found that the Harvard Admissions Office consistently rated Asian-Americans lower on personality traits such as "likability" and "kindness," even when they hadn't met with them in person. By contrast, alumni interviewers, who did meet the applicants, often rated them highly on personality.

Evidence: annual meetings of the Association of Black Admissions and Financial Aid Officers of the Ivy League and Sister Schools, or Abafaoilss, in which conferees share information about the race of their admitted and matriculated students. The Supreme Court has allowed race to be a consideration in admissions, while forbidding the kind of explicit racial balancing that seemed to be the purpose of the meetings.

All this confirms what most thoughtful people should know already about affirmative action: that what is supposed to be a powerful method for inclusion is an equally powerful method of exclusion. If you're going to say yes to Jack, you'll have to say no to Jill. The world of college admissions is a fixed pie.

What distinguishes the Harvard suit from past legal challenges to affirmative action is that it shows that the people the policy harms aren't privileged and unsympathetic white kids. The injured are other minorities.

Nor is this a matter of second-tier white students duking it out for the last available slots against standout minorities. The Asian-Americans rejected by Harvard are outstanding candidates being penalized by hoary stereotypes about having ferocious work ethics but not much else. Internal Harvard documents refer to them as "busy and bright" and "standard strong" — reminiscent of the way a previous generation of Jewish students were dismissed as "average geniuses" who were not "clubbable."

KAYANA SZYMCZAK FOR THE NEW YORK TIMES

Renee Gu, 7, rested during a rally in Copley Square to protest Harvard University's admissions practices toward Asian-Americans.

No wonder Harvard fought tooth-and-nail to keep those documents secret. The goal of achieving a desired racial composition on campus depends on Wizard of Oz-like schemes of dissembling and doublethink. The core problem with every noble lie is that it can only be concealed by an additional lie, then another. Whatever else it is, it's the opposite of Veritas.

Still, I can't help but think that critics of the plaintiffs are right in at least one respect: Those "busy and bright" kids who aren't going to Harvard will be fine. Most will still get into great schools and have good careers. They might rage against an institution that turned them away unfairly. Yet deep down they'll have the satisfaction of knowing their own worth.

Will that be equally true of those who, thanks to affirmative action, did get in? I wonder. Perhaps the deepest damage affirmative action does is to those it embraces, not those it rejects. It isn't a pleasant thing to live with the sense that your achievements aren't quite real — and that everyone secretly knows it. It's corrosive to live in the clutch of someone else's lie.

"The way to stop discrimination on the basis of race is to stop discriminating on the basis of race," John Roberts once wrote. Should this case reach the Supreme Court, let's hope he still means it.

BRET STEPHENS is an Op-Ed columnist for The New York Times.

Challengers of Affirmative Action Have a New Target: New York City's Elite High Schools

BY ELIZA SHAPIRO | DEC. 14, 2018

The controversy surrounding Mayor Bill de Blasio's plan to integrate the city's specialized high schools just intensified.

MAYOR BILL DE BLASIO'S PLAN to enroll more black and Hispanic students in New York City's most sought-after high schools faces a brand-new obstacle.

This week, the Pacific Legal Foundation, a conservative, libertarian-leaning law firm that has a history of challenging affirmative action policies, filed the first lawsuit against his admissions reform proposal, which he announced this summer.

But the suit does not take on the part of Mr. de Blasio's proposal that has provoked the most controversy: a plan that would entirely eliminate the exam that is currently the sole means of admission into the city's elite specialized high schools. The mayor wants to replace the test with a system that guarantees seats to top performers at each of the city's middle schools, which would guarantee that the schools accept many more black and Hispanic students.

Instead, Pacific Legal is taking aim at the first, and more modest, phase of Mr. de Blasio's proposal: the expansion of a program known as Discovery.

There is a key difference between the two phases: The city has the power to change Discovery by itself, but scrapping the test would require a change to state law in Albany.

WHAT IS DISCOVERY, EXACTLY?

Currently, specialized schools enroll tiny percentages of black and

Hispanic students, even though those students make up about 70 percent of the school system. This past year, only 10 black students were offered seats at Stuyvesant High School, the most competitive of the eight test-in specialized schools.

Discovery allows mostly low-income students who just miss the cutoff for entry to enroll in summer classes aimed at preparing them for the schools' academic rigor.

The current version of Discovery sets aside 6 percent of seats at specialized high schools for students who come from low-income families. Mr. de Blasio's plan would expand that to 20 percent of seats at each specialized school, and require schools to reserve seats for more vulnerable students who not only come from low-income families but also attend high-poverty schools.

In a twist, some of the fiercest critics of Mr. de Blasio's plan to scrap the admissions test are also the strongest backers of the push to expand Discovery.

The schools' powerful alumni groups have long been seen as a key obstacle to dramatic admissions reform. But as political pressure has grown around the issue in the last few months, those groups have faced fresh questions about how to integrate the schools. Discovery, which relies on the existence of the test to function, is their solution.

Soo H. Kim, the president of Stuyvesant High School's alumni organization, said: "Done the right way, Discovery is the answer. Full stop."

WHY FILE A SUIT?

Mr. de Blasio's plan calls for a sharp increase in the number of students filling seats through Discovery this year. But Joshua Thompson, the lead attorney on Pacific Legal's lawsuit, said he wants to maintain the status quo.

The complaint, filed in Federal District Court in Manhattan, has two parts: a lawsuit challenging the constitutionality of Discovery and a motion for a preliminary injunction.

Pacific Legal is asserting that, because Discovery could prevent some Asian-American students from gaining access to the schools, the program's expansion violates students' constitutional right to equal protection under the law. The expansion "has both a discriminatory purpose and effect," a Pacific Legal news release reads.

Mr. Thompson hopes the injunction will essentially block Discovery from expanding before applicants receive their admissions offers this spring.

"If the court grants an injunction, the specialized schools would look like they did last year," Mr. Thompson said in an interview.

The broader suit, Mr. Thompson said, could take "months or years" to resolve.

The city is standing behind its plan to expand Discovery, which would double the number of seats at specialized schools offered to black and Hispanic students, from about 9 percent to 16 percent.

"Our reforms will expand opportunity and raise the bar at our specialized high schools," Will Mantell, a spokesman for the Department of Education, said.

HOW DOES THE SUIT RELATE TO OTHER LEGAL CHALLENGES AGAINST AFFIRMATIVE ACTION?

Pacific Legal's lawsuit compounds a growing legal threat to affirmative action policies at selective schools.

This fall, representatives for Harvard University defended the school's admissions policies in a high-profile suit revolving around a similar question: Do elite schools use policies to enroll more black and Hispanic students at expense of Asian-American applicants?

Natasha Warikoo, a professor of education at Harvard who studies affirmative action, sees some parallels between the two lawsuits.

"There's this narrative of Asian-Americans being targeted in the quest to bring more opportunity to black and Latino people," she said. "I think that narrative is incredibly problematic."

Of Discovery, she said, "this is not crafted to exclude poor Asian kids."

One of the plaintiffs in Pacific Legal's case, the Asian-American Coalition for Education, has been sharply critical of Harvard's affirmative action policies for years. Other plaintiffs include Asian-American students who feel their entry to a specialized school could be blocked by the expansion of Discovery; the plaintiffs in Harvard's lawsuit are a group of Asian-American students who were rejected by Harvard.

AND WHAT ABOUT GETTING RID OF THE TEST?

This week's lawsuit presents a potential legal headache, but Mr. de Blasio's plan to eliminate the specialized high school exam has a much bigger problem: a glaring lack of political support.

The mayor wants to replace the exam with an admissions system that would offer seats to the top seven percent of students at each of the city's middle schools, according to their grades and test scores.

But as top city officials have taken that plan on the road this fall, presenting the proposal in each of the city's 32 school districts, they have been faced with criticism from all sides.

In Manhattan's District 2, which includes wealthy, mostly white neighborhoods like the Upper East Side and West Village, hundreds of parents shouted down officials at a recent meeting. Across the city, in the mostly black Brooklyn neighborhood of Bedford-Stuyvesant, parents at two meetings on the topic said the specialized school plan amounted to a distraction from larger problems in the city's schools.

The plan faces increasingly steep odds in Albany. This week, newly-elected State Senator John C. Liu of Queens, who has been outspoken against Mr. de Blasio's plan, was named the chairman of the Senate's New York City education committee. Michael Mulgrew, president of the United Federation of Teachers, which is a key player in Albany politics, has cast doubt on the plan's chances at the Capitol, and few if any politicians at the city or state level have been eager to take on the issue.

The legislative session will begin in January.

ELIZA SHAPIRO is a reporter covering New York City education. She joined The Times in 2018. Eliza grew up in New York City and attended public and private schools in Manhattan and Brooklyn.

Do American Women Still Need an Equal Rights Amendment?

ANALYSIS | BY SUSAN CHIRA | FEB. 16, 2019

We're already living in Phyllis Schlafly's nightmare.

WHEN PHYLLIS SCHLAFLY crusaded against the Equal Rights Amendment in the 1970s as a threat to all-American motherhood, she handed out freshly baked bread and apple pie to state legislators. She warned of a dystopian post-E.R.A. future of women forced to enlist in the military, gay marriage, unisex toilets everywhere and homemakers driven into the workplace by husbands free to abandon them.

The E.R.A., which had been sailing to ratification, failed. Yet gay marriage is now the law. Women in the military see combat, although women are not required to register for the draft. Six women — so far — are running for president. A record-shattering number of women have claimed seats in Congress. And the percentage of prime-working-age women participating in the labor force has soared from 51 percent in 1972, when Congress passed the E.R.A., to more than 75 percent last year.

So what protections did American women earn without a constitutional amendment? Did the country get everywhere the people pushing for the amendment wanted it to go? These questions, once theoretical, are newly relevant with a push to revive the Equal Rights Amendment. It was left for dead in 1982, when three states failed to ratify it by a congressionally imposed deadline, leaving it short of the necessary three fourths of the states needed for ratification. But in the past two years, Nevada and Illinois have ratified the amendment. In Virginia, campaigners are pushing the state to ratify the amendment before the legislative session ends on Feb. 23, though ratification is a long shot.

Mrs. Schlafly may not have been able to prevent social changes that transformed the lives of American women, but she did drive a wedge between conservatives and liberals that remains today. "She was one

BILL PIERCE/THE LIFE IMAGES COLLECTION/GETTY IMAGES

Phyllis Schlafly, here in 1976, predicted terrible things if the Equal Rights Amendment was ratified, including same-sex marriage and unisex toilets.

of the early architects of class conflict as expressed through culture wars, as a way to stop the progress of the equality ideals of the professional management elite," said Joan C. Williams, a feminist legal scholar skeptical about the usefulness of the Equal Rights Amendment. "One of the ironic messages of the E.R.A. is not to underestimate the power of 'bathroom anxiety' in pushing the country to the right."

Some of the very arguments Mrs. Schlafly deployed decades ago resurfaced in the recent state legislature debates. In Nevada, Illinois and Virginia, conservative women denounced the amendment. Women already have equal rights, and an amendment would take away remaining privileges, they argued. It would make it illegal to separate the sexes in bathrooms, college dormitories or school sports, they claimed. Women would lose programs like food subsidies aimed at mothers and female-only scholarships.

What the E.R.A. would change and what it would not is both bitterly contested and hypothetical. During the 1970s and 80s, a determined corps of lawyers led by Ruth Bader Ginsburg persuaded the Supreme Court to extend the equal protection clause of the 14th Amendment to cover many forms of sex discrimination. After the E.R.A. stalled, legislators passed a bevy of new laws. Together, these had the effect of opening new doors for women.

But advocates point to gaps in existing laws and Supreme Court decisions that have limited enforcement, particularly in the areas of violence against women, sexual harassment and equal pay.

Justice Ginsburg, speaking at the Aspen Institute in 2017, said that while women had come "almost as far" under the 14th Amendment as they would have under the E.R.A., she still believed an amendment had practical and symbolic value. "I would like to be able to take out my pocket Constitution and say that the equal citizenship stature of men and women is a fundamental tenet of our society like free speech," she said.

Catharine A. MacKinnon, whose legal theories laid the basis for sexual harassment being defined as a form of sex discrimination, has championed the revival of the amendment as a weapon against what she sees as the continuing subordination of women through sexual violence and economic inequality. "You go after sexuality and economics, you've gone to the heart of misogyny," she said.

The Violence Against Women Act, passed in 1994, originally allowed women to sue their attackers in federal court. This was an important provision because of wide variations in the way states prosecuted rape and sexual violence cases, said Erwin Chemerinsky, the dean of the University of California, Berkeley, law school. The Supreme Court struck down that part of the law in 2000. Many laws against discrimination, including the Civil Rights Act, are based on Congress's power to regulate interstate commerce, but the court ruled that did not apply in cases of sexual violence. This would change with an equal rights amendment, he said.

Attempts to remedy the persistent pay gap between men and women have also fallen short because of rulings saying that gaps must be the result of intentional discrimination in order to violate the law and that many differences in pay are the result of factors "other than sex," advocates say. If a woman doing the same work as a man is hired at a lower salary because her previous salary was lower, courts have ruled that is not pay discrimination, said Jessica Neuwirth, a co-founder of the E.R.A. Coalition. She believes an equal rights amendment would strengthen Congress's ability to remedy unequal pay.

The E.R.A. was a touchstone of cultural anxiety when it first ran aground. If the move to renew it gained real traction, would it affect today's most bitterly fought culture wars?

That, like so many things, depends on the conservative-liberal balance of the Supreme Court. Laws that restrict reproductive freedom obviously have a disparate impact on women, Mr. Chemerinsky said, but the court would have to decide whether such laws amount to discrimination on the basis of sex.

And our understanding of gender has changed in ways unimagined either by the suffragists who first drafted an equal rights amendment when women won the vote a century ago or the backers of the E.R.A. a half-century later. A real push for this amendment now might affect the treatment of trans people and who is legally seen as a man or a woman.

Ms. Williams, the legal scholar, believes the conservative tenor of the current court means justices would choose the narrowest interpretations of an equal rights amendment. Transformative change would be out of reach. Ms. Neuwirth argues just the opposite.

"It's almost more important in times like these to have very explicit constitutional language," she said. "If the law says no discrimination on the basis of sex, then no matter what your legal ideology as a judge, the more concrete the language is, the better off people are going to be."

SUSAN CHIRA is a senior correspondent and editor covering gender issues, and was part of a team that won a Pulitzer Prize in 2018 for public service for reporting on workplace sexual harassment issues.

Glossary

affirmative action A set of laws or policies that favor disenfranchised groups of people in efforts to make up for the discriminatory practices of the past.

bias Unfair policies or judgment instigated from prejudice based on characteristics such as race, age or gender.

civil rights Americans' rights to freedom and equality.

discrimination The unjust treatment of a specific group of people based on particular characteristics such as age, race or gender.

Equal Employment Opportunity Commission (E.E.O.C.) A government organization that enforces policies to help eliminate discrimination in the hiring process of public and private companies.

Equal Rights Amendment (E.R.A.) Legislation that would have guaranteed Americans equal rights and law protections under the Constitution regardless of a person's gender.

executive order A directive ordered by the U.S. president that dictates internal operations of the government and has the force of law. This influences how the government will respond to particular issues and emergencies.

Fair Employment Practice Committee (F.E.P.C.) An organization created to prevent discrimination by organizations involved in war-related work, especially in the homefront industry producing armaments and machinery for World War II.

Fair Housing Act A civil rights act that makes it illegal for someone to deny selling or renting property to a person based on their race, age, gender, or similar discriminatory qualities.

National Association for the Advancement of Colored People (N.A.A.C.P.) A civil rights organization established to advance the political, educational, social and economic equality of rights.

National Labor Relations Board (N.L.R.B.) An agency that enforces fair labor practices and protect employees rights to assemble (private or unions).

National Urban League A civil rights advocacy group based in New York City that addresses discrimination against African-Americans.

Philadelphia Plan A program of the U.S. Labor Department in the 1960s designed to encourage more employment in the construction sector for African Americans.

race-based admissions The policy of using race as admission criteria designed to reduce discrimination in the admission process and increase minority representation on campuses.

racial quotas A mandatory percentage or number of people needed to be employed or admitted into public or private organizations based on race. Often used in college admission considerations.

reverse discrimination When members of a majority group are discriminated against in order to favor a minority or disenfranchised group.

segregation Separating or setting apart groups of people based on characteristics such as age, race or gender.

stereotype A generalized view of a group of people based on social perceptions of the group possessing particular characteristics.

union Also known as trade or labor union, this is an association of workers from a particular industry that forms to represent workers in negotiations for better pay, labor practices and protections.

U.S. Supreme Court The highest court of law in the United States. The Supreme Court, which has nine justices, is involved in appeal cases and acts as the final judge in constitutional and congressional law.

Media Literacy Terms

"Media literacy" refers to the ability to access, understand, critically assess and create media. The following terms are important components of media literacy, and they will help you critically engage with the articles in this title.

attribution The method by which a source is identified or by which facts and information are assigned to the person who provided them.

balance Principle of journalism that both perspectives of an argument should be presented in a fair way.

column A type of story that is a regular feature, often on a recurring topic, written by the same journalist, generally known as a columnist.

human interest story A type of story that focuses on individuals and how events or issues affect their lives, generally offering a sense of relatability to the reader.

impartiality Principle of journalism that a story should not reflect a journalist's bias and should contain balance.

intention The motive or reason behind something, such as the publication of a news story.

news story An article or style of expository writing that reports news, generally in a straightforward fashion and without editorial comment.

op-ed An opinion piece that reflects a prominent individual's opinion on a topic of interest.

source The origin of the information reported in journalism.

tone A manner of expression in writing or speech.

Media Literacy Questions

1. Identify the various sources cited in the article "Gains Are Made in Federal Drive for Negro Hiring" (on page 93). How does John Herbers attribute information to each of these sources in his article? How effective are his attributions in helping the reader identify his sources?

2. In "Between the Lines of the Affirmative Action Opinion" (on page 145), John Schwartz directly quotes justices of the Supreme Court. What are the strengths of the use of a direct quote as opposed to a paraphrase? What are the weaknesses?

3. Compare the headlines of "The Stakes in Bakke" (on page 103) and "N.A.A.C.P. Says Bakke Ruling Has Brought Cuts in Minority Plans" (on page 106). Which is a more compelling headline, and why? How could the less compelling headline be changed to better draw the reader's interest?

4. What type of story is "Even Break Urged for All Workers" (on page 26)? Can you identify another article in this collection that is the same type of story? What elements helped you come to your conclusion?

5. Does Thomas J. Espenshade demonstrate the journalistic principle of balance in his article "Moving Beyond Affirmative Action" (on page 141)? If so, how did he do so? If not, what could Espenshade have included to make his article more balanced?

6. The article "I'm for Affirmative Action. Can You Change My Mind?" (on page 181) is an example of an op-ed. Identify how Gary Gutting's attitude and tone help convey his opinion on the topic.

7. Does "Plans to Ease Hiring Rules Attacked" (on page 112) use multiple sources? What are the strengths of using multiple sources in a journalistic piece? What are the weaknesses of relying heavily on only one or a few sources?

8. "If Affirmative Action Is Doomed, What's Next?" (on page 185) features a graph and two photographs. What do these images add to the article?

9. What is the intention of the article "The Rest of the Ivy League Comes to Harvard's Aid in Admissions Challenge" (on page 168)? How effectively does it achieve its intended purpose?

10. Analyze the authors' reporting in "Supreme Court Upholds Affirmative Action Program at University of Texas" (on page 153) and "Challengers of Affirmative Action Have a New Target: New York City's Elite High Schools" (on page 204). Do you think one journalist is more balanced in their reporting than the other? If so, why do you think so?

11. Identify each of the sources in " 'Lopping,' 'Tips' and the 'Z-List': Bias Lawsuit Explores Harvard's Admissions Secrets" (on page 158) as a primary source or a secondary source. Evaluate the reliability and credibility of each source. How does your evaluation of each source change your perspective on this article?

Citations

All citations in this list are formatted according to the Modern Language Association's (MLA) style guide.

BOOK CITATION

THE NEW YORK TIMES EDITORIAL STAFF. *Affirmative Action: Still Necessary or Unfair Advantage?* New York Times Educational Publishing, 2021.

ONLINE ARTICLE CITATIONS

BENNER, KATIE. "Justice Dept. Backs Suit Accusing Harvard of Discriminating Against Asian-American Applicants." *The New York Times*, 30 Aug. 2018, https://www.nytimes.com/2018/08/30/us/politics/asian-students-affirmative-action-harvard.html.

CAMPBELL, COLIN. "Plans to Ease Hiring Rules Attacked." *The New York Times*, 26 Aug. 1981, https://timesmachine.nytimes.com/timesmachine/1981/08/26/247119.html.

CHIRA, SUSAN. "Do American Women Still Need an Equal Rights Amendment?" *The New York Times*, 16 Feb. 2019, https://www.nytimes.com/2019/02/16/sunday-review/women-equal-rights-amendment.html.

ESPENSHADE, THOMAS J. "Moving Beyond Affirmative Action." *The New York Times*, 4 Oct. 2012, https://www.nytimes.com/2012/10/05/opinion/moving-beyond-affirmative-action.html.

GREEN, ERICA L., ET AL. "Trump Officials Reverse Obama's Policy on Affirmative Action in Schools." *The New York Times*, 3 July 2018, https://www.nytimes.com/2018/07/03/us/politics/trump-affirmative-action-race-schools.html.

GREENHOUSE, LINDA. "Affirmative Action Ruling Is Called a Breakthrough." *The New York Times*, 4 July 1980, https://timesmachine.nytimes.com/timesmachine/1980/07/04/112152147.html.

GREENHOUSE, LINDA. "Justices, 5 to 4, Cast Doubts on U.S. Programs That

Give Preferences Based on Race." *The New York Times*, 13 June 1995, https://timesmachine.nytimes.com/timesmachine/1995/06/13/552595.html.

GREENHOUSE, LINDA. "Supreme Court Dismisses Challenge in Its Main Affirmative Action Case." *The New York Times*, 28 Nov. 2001, https://www.nytimes.com/2001/11/28/us/supreme-court-dismisses-challenge-in-its-main-affirmative-action-case.html.

GUTTING, GARY. "I'm for Affirmative Action. Can You Change My Mind?" *The New York Times*, 10 Dec. 2018, https://www.nytimes.com/2018/12/10/opinion/im-for-affirmative-action-can-you-change-my-mind.html.

HARTOCOLLIS, ANEMONA. "The Rest of the Ivy League Comes to Harvard's Aid in Admissions Challenge." *The New York Times*, 30 July 2018, https://www.nytimes.com/2018/07/30/us/ivy-league-harvard-admissions.html.

HARTOCOLLIS, ANEMONA. "What's at Stake in the Harvard Lawsuit? Decades of Debate Over Race in Admissions." *The New York Times*, 13 Oct. 2018, https://www.nytimes.com/2018/10/13/us/harvard-affirmative-action-asian-students.html.

HARTOCOLLIS, ANEMONA, ET AL. " 'Lopping,' 'Tips' and the 'Z-List': Bias Lawsuit Explores Harvard's Admissions Secrets." *The New York Times*, 29 July 2018, https://www.nytimes.com/2018/07/29/us/harvard-admissions-asian-americans.html.

HERBERS, JOHN. "Bans on Job Bias Effective Today." *The New York Times*, 2 July 1965, https://timesmachine.nytimes.com/timesmachine/1965/07/02/96703972.html.

HERBERS, JOHN. "Gains Are Made in Federal Drive for Negro Hiring." *The New York Times*, 25 Jan. 1970, https://timesmachine.nytimes.com/timesmachine/1970/01/25/91176877.html.

HUNTER, CHARLAYNE. "After Nine Years — A Homecoming for the First Black Girl at the University of Georiga." *The New York Times*, 25 Jan. 1970, https://timesmachine.nytimes.com/timesmachine/1970/01/25/91179289.html.

HUNTER, MARJORIE. "State Approves Civil Rights Bill By 71-to-20 Vote." *The New York Times*, 12 Mar. 1968, https://timesmachine.nytimes.com/timesmachine/1968/03/12/79935545.html.

JANSON, DONALD. "U.S. Judge Upholds Controversial Philadelphia Plan to Increase Hiring of Minorities in Building Industry." *The New York Times*, 15 Mar. 1970, https://timesmachine.nytimes.com/timesmachine/1970/03/15/93879502.html.

JOHNSON, JULIE. "Bush Vows Rights Effort on Jobs and Economic Development." *The New York Times*, 9 Aug. 1989, https://timesmachine.nytimes.com/timesmachine/1989/08/09/256689.html.

JOHNSON, JULIE. "Rights Panel Sees Decline in U.S. Enforcement." *The New York Times*, 18 Jan. 1989, https://timesmachine.nytimes.com/timesmachine/1989/01/18/114489.html.

JOHNSON, THOMAS A. "N.A.A.C.P. Says Bakke Ruling Has Brought Cuts in Minority Plans." *The New York Times*, 9 Jan. 1979, https://timesmachine.nytimes.com/timesmachine/1979/01/09/111067507.html.

KATZNELSON, IRA. "Making Affirmative Action White Again." *The New York Times*, 12 Aug. 2017, https://www.nytimes.com/2017/08/12/opinion/sunday/making-affirmative-action-white-again.html.

LAVINSKY, LARRY M. "The Dangers of Racial Quotas." *The New York Times*, 15 June 1977, https://timesmachine.nytimes.com/timesmachine/1977/06/15/355834222.html.

LEONHARDT, DAVID. "If Affirmative Action Is Doomed, What's Next?" *The New York Times*, 17 June 2014, https://www.nytimes.com/2014/06/17/upshot/if-affirmative-action-is-doomed-whats-next.html.

LEWIS, ANTHONY. "Kennedy Sets Pattern on Civil Rights." *The New York Times*, 12 Mar. 1961, https://timesmachine.nytimes.com/timesmachine/1961/03/12/100240666.html.

LEWIS, ANTHONY. "The Stakes in Bakke." *The New York Times*, 12 Sept. 1977, https://timesmachine.nytimes.com/timesmachine/1977/09/12/75301789.html.

LEWIS, NEIL A. "Administration Backs Affirmative Action Plan." *The New York Times*, 11 Aug. 2011, https://www.nytimes.com/2001/08/11/us/administration-backs-affirmative-action-plan.html.

LIPTAK, ADAM. "Supreme Court Upholds Affirmative Action Program at University of Texas." *The New York Times*, 23 June 2016, https://www.nytimes.com/2016/06/24/us/politics/supreme-court-affirmative-action-university-of-texas.html.

THE NEW YORK TIMES. "Bill for Equal Pay Offered in Senate." *The New York Times*, 22 June 1945, https://timesmachine.nytimes.com/timesmachine/1945/06/22/94020548.html.

THE NEW YORK TIMES. "Civil Rights Gain Reported by A.J.C." *The New York Times*, 5 Aug. 1959, https://timesmachine.nytimes.com/timesmachine/1959/08/05/80542058.html.

THE NEW YORK TIMES. "Equal Job Rights for Women Asked." *The New York Times*, 22 May 1938, https://timesmachine.nytimes.com/timesmachine/1938/05/22/99542412.html.

THE NEW YORK TIMES. "Even Break Urged for All Workers." *The New York Times*, 3 Sept. 1946, https://timesmachine.nytimes.com/timesmachine/1946/09/03/91098191.html.

THE NEW YORK TIMES. "Geneva Labor Body to Study Discrimination Against Employment of Aging Workers." *The New York Times*, 6 Feb. 1938, https://timesmachine.nytimes.com/timesmachine/1938/02/06/96795907.html.

THE NEW YORK TIMES. "Kennedy Statement and Executive Order on Equal Job Opportunity." *The New York Times*, 7 Mar. 1961, https://timesmachine.nytimes.com/timesmachine/1961/03/07/101450326.html.

THE NEW YORK TIMES. "New Board Set Up to End Hiring Bias." *The New York Times*, 29 May 1943, https://timesmachine.nytimes.com/timesmachine/1943/05/29/85104552.html.

THE NEW YORK TIMES. "Posts in Cabinet Urged for Women." *The New York Times*, 4 Dec. 1936, https://timesmachine.nytimes.com/timesmachine/1936/12/04/88715587.html.

THE NEW YORK TIMES. "President Orders an Even Break for Minorities in Defense Jobs." *The New York Times*, 26 June 1941, https://timesmachine.nytimes.com/timesmachine/1941/06/26/87634736.html.

THE NEW YORK TIMES. "Union Is Directed to Admit Negroes." *The New York Times*, 18 Aug. 1951, https://timesmachine.nytimes.com/timesmachine/1951/08/18/84682815.html.

THE NEW YORK TIMES. "Wagner Act Changes." *The New York Times*, 13 Aug. 1946, https://timesmachine.nytimes.com/timesmachine/1946/08/13/140133812.html.

OELSNER, LESLEY. "Court to Weigh College Admission That Gives Minorities Preference." *The New York Times*, 23 Feb. 1977, https://timesmachine.nytimes.com/timesmachine/1977/02/23/80192636.html.

POMFRET, JOHN D. "President Urges Congress to Ban All Housing Bias." *The New York Times*, 29 Apr. 1966, https://timesmachine.nytimes.com/timesmachine/1966/04/29/79291879.html.

REED, ROY. "New U.S. Job Plan for Negroes Set." *The New York Times*, 18 July 1969, https://timesmachine.nytimes.com/timesmachine/1969/07/18/78386772.html.

SAUL, STEPHANIE. "Colleges That Ask Applicants About Brushes With the

Law Draw Scrutiny." *The New York Times*, 28 Jan. 2016, https://www.nytimes.com/2016/01/29/us/colleges-that-ask-applicants-about-brushes-with-the-law-draw-scrutiny.html.

SCHWARTZ, JOHN. "Between the Lines of the Affirmative Action Opinion." *The New York Times*, 24 June 2013, https://archive.nytimes.com/www.nytimes.com/interactive/2013/06/24/us/annotated-supreme-court-decision-on-affirmative-action.html.

SEMPLE, ROBERT B., JR. "Philadelphia Plan: How White House Engineered Major Victory." *The New York Times*, 26 Dec. 1969, https://timesmachine.nytimes.com/timesmachine/1969/12/26/88875632.html.

SHAPIRO, ELIZA. "Challengers of Affirmative Action Have a New Target: New York City's Elite High Schools." *The New York Times*, 14 Dec. 2018, https://www.nytimes.com/2018/12/14/nyregion/affirmative-action-lawsuit-nyc-high-schools.html.

STARK, LOUIS. "Warns Railroads on Negro Job Ban." *The New York Times*, 1 Dec. 1943, https://timesmachine.nytimes.com/timesmachine/1943/12/01/85137917.html.

STEPHENS, BRET. "The Curse of Affirmative Action." *The New York Times*, 19 Oct. 2018, https://www.nytimes.com/2018/10/19/opinion/harvard-case-affirmative-action.html.

Index

A

academia
- admission processes and minorities, 133–137, 141–144, 145–148, 153–157, 158–167
- admission questions about criminal history, 149–152
- Harvard, and claim of Asian-American discrimination, 158–167, 168–170, 171–175, 176–180, 196, 200–202, 206
- and racial quotas, 138–140

Adarand Constructors v. Mineta, 129–132

Adarand Constructors v. Peña, 121–125, 126, 130

African-Americans
- and Civil Rights Act of 1964, 8, 52–56, 58, 66, 68, 72, 94, 100, 101, 110, 181, 210
- civil rights gained reported by American Jewish Congress, 32–33
- and employment discrimination by railroads, 21–23
- and gains in federal hiring, 93–99
- and International Brotherhood of Electrical Workers, 30–31
- Kennedy executive order on equal job opportunity, 34–47, 48–51
- and legislation banning housing bias, 57–60
- and the Philadelphia Plan, 65–66, 67–73, 93–94, 95, 96, 100–102
- Roosevelt executive orders on discrimination in defense jobs, 18–19, 20

Alito, Samuel A., Jr., 154, 155, 156, 157, 179

Allen, William Barclay, 119–120

Allott, Gorden, 72

American Jewish Congress, 32

Anderson, Mary, 25

Ashcroft, John, 127, 128

Asian-Americans, and claim of discrimination in Harvard's admission process, 158–167, 168–170, 171–175, 176–180, 196, 200–202, 206

Auburn University, admission questions about criminal history, 149–152

B

Bacow, Lawrence, 179–180

Baldwin, Joseph Clark, 12

Barney, Clarence L., 119

Baude, William, 178, 179

Bhargava, Anurima, 198

Biemiller, Andrew, 70–71

Blum, Edward, 160, 169, 170, 174, 179

Brandenburg, John P., 112, 113, 114

Brennan, William J., Jr., 134

Breyer, Stephen G., 124, 132, 154

Broekhuizen, Kim, 198

Bush, George H. W./Bush administration, 115, 117–120

Bush, George W./Bush administration, 126–128, 131, 193, 194, 197

C

Carter, Jimmy, 105, 114

City of Richmond v. Croson, 125

Civil Rights Act of 1964, 8, 52–56, 58, 66, 68, 72, 94, 100, 101, 110, 181, 210

civil rights movement, 8, 30, 93, 160

Clegg, Roger, 153, 196, 198–199

Clinton, Bill/Clinton administration, 123, 126, 127, 130, 131, 169

Colebert, Ben, 80, 81, 82,

83, 86–87
Committee on Equal Employment Opportunity, 34–47
Committee on Fair Employment Practice, 18, 20, 21, 24

D

De Blasio, Bill, 204–207
DeVos, Betsy, 195, 199
Discovery program, 204–207

E

Ehrlichman, John, 69, 70, 134
Eisenhower, Dwight D./Eisenhower administration, 49, 51, 115
Equal Employment Opportunity Commission, 52, 58, 94
Equal Rights Amendment, 208–211
Ervin, Sam J., 59, 96–97

F

Fifteenth Amendment, 33
Fisher, Abigail, 141, 155, 156
Fisher v. University of Texas, 141–144, 145–148, 153–157, 160, 179, 193, 194, 197, 199
Fitzsimmons, William, 162, 165
Flemming, Arthur S., 115
Fletcher, Arthur, 65, 71, 72
Forbes-Watson, John, 14
Ford, Gerald R., 63, 72
Fourteenth Amendment, 33, 210
Fullilove v. Klutznick, 109–111, 123, 124
"Future of Affirmative Action, The," 188

G

Garment, Leonard, 67, 69–70, 71, 73
Georgia, University of, 74–92
Ginsburg, Ruth Bader, 124, 132, 145, 147, 154, 210
Grutter v. Bollinger, 141, 144, 145, 147, 155, 193, 194

H

Harvard, and claim of Asian-American discrimination, 158–167, 168–170, 171–175, 176–180, 196, 200–202, 206
Holmes, Hamilton "Hamp," 74, 76, 77, 80, 85, 91, 92
Hooks, Benjamin, 8, 106–107, 108, 112, 113
Hughes, Chuck, 163–164, 166
Hull, Helen, 12
Hunter, Charlayne, 74–92

I

International Brotherhood of Electrical Workers, 30–31
International Labor Organization, 13, 25

J

Jackson, Melodie, 197
Jacob, John E., 118
Javits, Jacob K., 64, 67
Johnson, Lyndon/Johnson administration, 7, 49, 52, 53, 55, 57–60, 61, 101, 125
Jones, Nathaniel, 106, 107, 108

K

Kagan, Elena, 145, 154
Kavanaugh, Brett M., 174, 179
Kennedy, Anthony M., 122, 132, 145, 146, 153, 154, 155–156, 175, 190, 195, 197
Kennedy, John F./Kennedy administration, 7–8, 57, 199
  executive order on equal job opportunity, 34–47, 48–51
Kennedy, Robert, 50
Khurana, Rakesh, 159–160, 167
Kiley, Robert, 103, 104
King, Martin Luther, Jr., 58, 71, 78, 115, 160

L

LeSourde, Howard M., 12
Lhamon, Catherine, 198
Lucas, William C., 117, 119

M

MacKinnon, Catharine A., 210
Marcus, Kenneth L., 199
Marshall, Thurgood, 122, 125, 134, 187
Metro Broadcasting v. F.C.C., 123
Mitchell, John N., 68, 69, 72

N

National Association for the Advancement of Colored People (N.A.A.C.P.), 58, 71, 81, 99, 106–108, 110, 112, 157, 168, 170, 173
National Labor Relations

Board, 28, 29
New Deal, 7, 10, 191, 192
New York City specialized high schools, plan for more minorities in, 204–207
Nixon, Richard/Nixon administration, 67–73, 93, 97, 101, 134

O

Obama, Barack/Obama administration, 9, 153–154, 173, 175, 177, 185, 195–199
O'Connor, Sandra Day, 121, 122, 123, 124, 132, 144, 155

P

Pelosi, Nancy, 196
Pendley, William Perry, 131
Philadelphia Plan, 65–66, 67–73, 93–94, 95, 96, 100–102
physical handicaps, 26–27
"Place, Not Race," 187

Q

quotas, 9, 66, 68, 72, 94, 95, 96–97, 100, 101, 127, 133, 138–140, 174, 176, 178, 185, 199, 200

R

railroads, and discrimination, 21–23
Rauh, Joseph, Jr., 59, 71, 72, 73
Reagan, Ronald/Reagan administration, 112–114, 115–116, 117, 118
Rehnquist, William H., 122, 132, 136
Reilly, Gerard D., 28–29
reverse discrimination, 93, 133
Roberts, John G., Jr., 156, 179, 181, 182, 183, 186, 203
Roosevelt, Franklin D., 7, 10, 18–19, 20, 21

S

Sales, Joe, 85, 91
Scalia, Antonin, 122, 132, 145, 146
Schindler, Miriam Albee, 16
Schlafly, Phyllis, 208–209
Schwellenbach, Lewis B., 26–27
Sessions, Jeff, 174, 191, 198
Shapiro, Ilya, 179
Shultz, George P., 66, 69, 71, 72, 96, 100
Sims, O. Suthern, 76, 77, 78–80
Sotomayor, Sonia, 154, 182–183
Souter, David H., 124, 125, 132
Staats, Elmer B., 68, 69, 95, 101
Stevens, John Paul, 124–125, 132

T

Thomas, Clarence, 122, 132, 145, 147, 156
Trump, Donald/Trump administration, 9, 172, 174, 175, 177, 185, 194, 195–199, 200

U

unions, 8, 18, 21, 22, 23, 28, 29, 30–31, 39, 41, 42, 44, 50, 53, 54, 67, 68, 72, 94, 95, 96, 97, 98, 101, 191, 192
U.S. Supreme Court, 59, 117, 126–128, 133–137, 138–140, 172, 174, 177, 178, 185, 195, 196, 197, 201, 203, 210, 211
  Adarand Constructors v. Mineta, 129–132
  Adarand Constructors v. Peña, 121–125, 126, 130
  City of Richmond v. Croson, 125
  Fisher v. University of Texas, 141–144, 145–148, 153–157, 160, 179, 193, 194, 197, 199
  Fullilove v. Klutznick, 109–111, 123, 124
  Grutter v. Bollinger, 141, 144, 145, 147, 155, 193, 194
  University of California v. Bakke, 103–105, 106–108, 109, 110, 133–137, 138–140, 145, 146, 194

W

Wagner Act, 7, 28–29, 192
Warikoo, Natasha, 206–207
Weiner, Charles R., 100–102
White, Byron R., 134
Wilcox, James, 192
Wilkins, Roy, 58, 71
women
  equal pay bill for wartime women workers, 24–25
  and Equal Rights Amendment, 208–211
  resolutions adopted by the State Federation of Business and Professional Women, 15–17
  and urge for cabinet posts, 10–12

This book is current up until the time of printing. For the most up-to-date reporting, visit www.nytimes.com.